THE ABUNDANT LIFE
BIBLE
AMPLIFIER

JAMES

Exodus   **Jon L. Dybdahl**
God Creates a People
Samuel   **Alden Thompson**
From the Danger of Chaos to the Danger of Power
Daniel 1–7   **William H. Shea**
Prophecy As History
Daniel 7–12   **William H. Shea**
Prophecies of the End Time
Hosea–Micah   **Jon L. Dybdahl**
A Call to Radical Reform
Matthew   **George R. Knight**
The Gospel of the Kingdom
John   **Jon Paulien**
Jesus Gives Life to a New Generation
Romans   **John C. Brunt**
Mercy for All
Timothy & Titus   **Charles E. Bradford**
Counsels to Young Pastors for Struggling Churches
Hebrews   **William G. Johnsson**
Full Assurance for Christians Today
Peter & Jude   **Robert M. Johnston**
Living in Dangerous Times

PEDRITO U. MAYNARD-REID, Th.D.

THE ABUNDANT LIFE
BIBLE
AMPLIFIER

JAMES

**True Religion
in Suffering**

GEORGE R. KNIGHT
General Editor

Pacific Press Publishing Association
Boise, Idaho
Oshawa, Ontario, Canada

Edited by B. Russell Holt
Designed by Tim Larson

Copyright © 1996 by
Pacific Press Publishing Association
Printed in the United States of America
All Rights Reserved

Maynard-Reid, Pedrito U.
  James : true religion in suffering / Pedrito U. Maynard-Reid.
    p.   cm. — (The abundant life Bible amplifier)
  Includes bibliographical references.
  ISBN 0-8163-1379-2 (hard : alk. paper). — ISBN 0-8163-1380-6 (paper : alk. paper)
  1. Bible. N.T. James—Criticism, interpretation, etc. I. Title. II. Series
BS2785.2.M29 1996
227' .9107—dc20   96-41897
                                                          CIP

96 97 98 99 00 • 5 4 3 2 1

CONTENTS

For Audrey, whose pediatric care for suffering children
places her in the apostolic line of James.

GENERAL PREFACE

The Abundant Life Bible Amplifier series is aimed at helping readers understand the Bible better. Rather than merely offering comments on or about the Bible, each volume seeks to enable people to study their Bibles with fuller understanding.

To accomplish that task, scholars who are also proven communicators have been selected to author each volume. The basic idea underlying this combination is that scholarship and the ability to communicate on a popular level are compatible skills.

While the Bible Amplifier is written with the needs and abilities of laypeople in mind, it will also prove helpful to pastors and teachers. Beyond individual readers, the series will be useful in church study groups and as guides to enrich participation in the weekly prayer meeting.

Rather than focusing on the details of each verse, the Bible Amplifier series seeks to give readers an understanding of the themes and patterns of each biblical book as a whole and how each passage fits into that context. As a result, the series does not seek to solve all the problems or answer all the questions that may be related to a given text. In the process of accomplishing the goal for the series, both inductive and explanatory methodologies are used.

Each volume in this series presents its author's understanding of the biblical book being studied. As such, it does not necessarily represent the "official" position of the Seventh-day Adventist Church.

It should be noted that the Bible Amplifier series utilizes the New International Version of the Bible as its basic text. *Every reader should read the "How to Use This Book" section to get the fullest benefit from the Bible Amplifier study volumes.*

Dr. Pedrito Maynard-Reid teaches New Testament at Walla Walla College. Prior to his present position he taught at West Indies College in Jamaica and Antillian University in Puerto Rico. His doctrinal dissertation was on the book of James and he is the author of *Poverty and Wealth in James*.

George R. Knight
Berrien Springs, Michigan

AUTHOR'S PREFACE

The invitation by George Knight and Pacific Press to write this commentary on the Epistle of James elicited mixed feelings. There was a feeling of inadequacy. Could I produce a book that would be scholarly sound and at the same time readable and "soul-inspiring"? But there was also a feeling of joy that I could share the blessings this marvelous book has given me—from my childhood days at my godly mother's feet even until now in the halls of academia and behind the pastoral lectern.

This journey of blessings was intensified when I wrote my doctoral dissertation on James's discussion of the poor and the rich in his epistle. Then I discovered in new ways an apostle who was practical yet deeply theological. James's theology had its roots in ministry, ethical pastoral concern, and "prophetic" challenge. He, like the ancient prophets, challenged his readers to a higher standard of godly living. But his pastoral sensitivities were for those in his community who were undergoing trials and sufferings of various kinds. To them he gave hope. This challenge and hope is as relevant today as it was 2,000 years ago.

This volume would not be what it is without the assistance and support of a number of persons. I am grateful to Walla Walla College, and particularly to my colleagues in the School of Theology, for granting me a sabbatical to do much of the work on this manuscript. But it was their genuine prayers, care, and loving support that spurred me on.

My sister, Dr. Audrey Reid, has been an inspiration and source of wisdom and strength. The fact that she and her husband, Lee, provided room and board in sunny California during my winter sabbatical is the least of the things for which I owe her a debt. Her personal, special, individual pediatric care and concern for children truly places her in the line of James, whose concern was for the suffering ones—

11

whether they were sick, poor, or otherwise in pain. Because of Audrey's positive influence on my life and ministry, I dedicated this volume to her.

Lorraine Jacobs has been a faith cheerleader for my academic exploits. But she has done more. Her editing, typing, and critiquing have enormously improved the drafts of this commentary. For her countless hours of sacrificial labor I owe her an enormous debt of gratitude.

My dear wife, Violet, has had more than the "patience of Job." She endured not only my absence for a three-month sabbatical, but (when I was at home) she accepted, without complaint, my domestic absent-mindedness as I researched and wrote. For her constant tolerance, support, and encouragement, I give God thanks and praise her name eternally.

My hope and prayer is that the reader of this volume will be enriched as he or she wrestles with the text of James. I trust that new and fresh perspectives will be gained that will not only bring about intellectual growth but will draw him or her closer to Christ and their neighbors.

How to Use This Book

The Abundant Life Amplifier series treats each major portion of each Bible book in five main sections.

The first section is called "Getting Into the Word." The purpose of this section is to encourage readers to study their own Bibles. For that reason, the text of the Bible has not been printed in the volumes in this series.

You will get the most out of your study if you work through the exercises in each of the "Getting Into the Word" sections. This will not only aid you in learning more about the Bible but will also increase your skill in using Bible tools and in asking (and answering) meaningful questions about the Bible.

It will be helpful if you write out the answers and keep them in a notebook or file folder for each biblical book. Writing out your thoughts will enhance your understanding. The benefit derived from such study, of course, will be proportionate to the amount of effort expended.

The "Getting Into the Word" sections assume that the reader has certain minimal tools available. Among these are a concordance and a Bible with maps and marginal cross-references. If you don't have a New International Version of the Bible, we recommend that you obtain one for use with this series, since all the Bible Amplifier authors are using the NIV as their basic text. For the same reason, your best choice of a concordance is the *NIV Exhaustive Concordance*, edited by E. W. Goodrick and J. R. Kohlenberger. *Strong's Exhaustive Concordance of the Bible* and *Young's Analytical Concordance to the Bible* are also useful. However, even if all you have is *Cruden's Complete Concordance*, you will be able to do all the "Getting Into the Word" exercises and most of the "Researching the Word" exercises.

The "Getting Into the Word" sections also assume that the reader has a Bible dictionary. The *Seventh-day Adventist Bible Dictionary* is quite helpful, but those interested in greater depth may want to acquire the four-volume *International Standard Bible Encyclopedia* (1974-1988 edition) or the six-volume *Anchor Bible Dictionary*.

The second section in the treatment of the biblical passages is called "Exploring the Word." The purpose of this section is to discuss the major themes in each biblical book. Thus the comments will typically deal with fairly large portions of Scripture (often an entire chapter) rather than providing a verse-by-verse treatment, such as is found in the *Seventh-day Adventist Bible Commentary*. In fact, many verses and perhaps whole passages in some biblical books may be treated minimally or passed over altogether.

Another thing that should be noted is that the purpose of the "Exploring the Word" sections is not to respond to all the problems or answer all the questions that might arise in each passage. Rather, as stated above, the "Exploring the Word" sections are to develop the Bible writers' major themes. In the process, the author of each volume will bring the best of modern scholarship into the discussion and thus enrich the reader's understanding of the biblical passage at hand. The "Exploring the Word" sections will also develop and provide insight into many of the issues first raised in the "Getting Into the Word" exercises.

The third section in the treatment of the biblical passage is "Applying the Word." This section is aimed at bringing the lessons of each passage into daily life. Once again, you may want to write out a response to these questions and keep them in your notebook or file folder on the biblical book being studied.

The fourth section, "Researching the Word," is for those students who want to delve more deeply into the Bible passage under study or into the history behind it. It is recognized that not everyone will have the research tools for this section. Those expecting to use the research sections should have an exhaustive Bible concordance, the *Seventh-day Adventist Bible Commentary*, a good Bible dictionary, and a Bible atlas. It will also be helpful to have several versions of the Bible.

The final component in each chapter of this book will be a list of recommendations for "Further Study of the Word." While most readers will not have all of these works, many of them may be available in local libraries. Others can be purchased through your local book dealer. It is assumed that many users of this series will already own the seven-volume *Seventh-day Adventist Bible Commentary* and the one-volume *Seventh-day Adventist Bible Dictionary*.

In closing, it should be noted that while a reader will learn much about the Bible from a *reading* of the books in the Bible Amplifier series, he or she will gain infinitely more by *studying* the Bible in connection with that reading.

The Epistle of James

My first childhood recollection of this epistle as an entire biblical document was hearing my aunt Beryl repeat it from memory at our home in Kingston, Jamaica. But for her, as for the rest of my family and extended family, it was not just another literary piece to repeat. The epistle was for us a special document that was most important in our Christian character formation and significantly affected our behavior. It was a guidebook; though not a legalistic code book. In its five brief chapters, the Epistle of James sets forth basic guidelines that aided us in our moral and ethical development and growth.

The following assignments are intended to help you begin to experience the power of James's letter. Before you begin, pray that God will assist you in grasping the magnificence of the book and also aid you in your moral and ethical development and growth.

1. **Read through James, not once or twice but numerous times. Read it aloud at least one of the times. (Listening to an oral recording of the book is also helpful.) Become familiar with the epistle.**
2. **Before reading this Introduction, attempt to make an outline of the epistle based on your reading of the text.**
3. **In a good Bible dictionary or Bible encyclopedia, read the articles on "James" or "The Epistle of James." This can prove profitable in ascertaining the historical background of the book.**

4. In a notebook, reserved for your study of the epistle, list four or five major passages from James's letter that have been significant to you in the past. Why did you choose these verses? How have they continued to influence your life?

5. List three or four texts or passages in James that you find difficult to understand or to relate to personally. Jot down the reasons why you find them problematic or why they seem to create a dilemma.

6. As you read through this epistle, did you see one particular theme that ran through the book? Jot it down in your notebook. List specific passages in which that theme is prominent.

7. List five or six verses in which James gives hope to those who are undergoing trials and sufferings.

Although James has been a marvelous little document to me, it has not enjoyed that status in the history of Christianity. John Elliot notes that it is "customarily ranked among the 'junk mail' of the Second Testament" (71). There are a number of reasons for this. First, even as far back as the second, third, and fourth centuries A.D., James had difficulty gaining status in the canon. The possible reason is that it was an embarrassment to some wealthy Christians who saw in the epistle what they believed were unnecessarily harsh criticism of their lifestyle, as well as its unqualified support of the poor (Blondel, 256).

Second, probably the most significant reason for James's negative press is Martin Luther's evaluation of the book. He held James, Jude, Hebrews, and Revelation to be secondary to such books as the Gospel of John, Paul's epistles (especially Romans and Galatians), and 1 Peter. These latter books, he claimed, manifested and upheld Christ clearly. These letters of John, Paul, and Peter instructed Christians in everything that was essential for their salvation. Even if Christians should never read or hear anything else from any other biblical book or any other teaching, they would have the fundamentals of evangelical Christianity from the writings of those three apostles. In comparison with these, James was an epistle of straw, according to Luther. It contained nothing of the gospel; it was not evangelical (i.e., it was not based on the freedom of the gospel); it was legalistic. Luther didn't quite throw it out of his canon, but he relegated it to the very back of the Bible.

Protestant Bible students have been so influenced by this great Reformer that they, like Luther, continue to hold up James against the yardstick of Paul. And because James does not seem to delve into such great theological themes as justification by faith, atonement, and other aspects of Christology and soteriology, James is weighed in the balance and found wanting.

The problem, however, is not with James; it is with us, his readers and interpreters. We have placed an artificial hierarchy on theological reflection, arguing that some issues and themes are heavyweight and theological, while others are lightweight and practical. We see the former as being superior to the latter. But in reality, both theological reflection and practical religion are equally important in our total growth. All aspects of theology—whether they be doctrinal, dry academics, or practical ethics—are essential to the Christian's character formation.

Very few will deny that James is possibly the most practical book (without downplaying its theological character) in the New Testament. But the letter reads like one of the books of the prophets, such as Isaiah, Jeremiah, Hosea, or Amos. James has a prophetic ring of challenge and confrontation similar to that pervading those Old Testament books. Yet, even though James reads like a "prophetic" book, it is loaded with pastoral encouragement. The author is clearly a true pastor who does not remain aloof from the everyday existence of his community. He is not an ivory-tower theologian. Rather, he is a task-oriented theologian; that is, he is a theologian; whose practical theology grows out of his ministry of labor and work in the day-by-day life of his people.

The Epistle of James is a model manual for pastors, church leaders, and all members today. Paul Cedar calls it a "how-to-do-it-manual" (11). Even though it may not speak directly and precisely to every issue the contemporary Christian faces, the subjects dealt with in the document are as relevant for us as they were to James's readers nearly 2,000 years ago.

In an age when there is much talk about personal and corporate renewal—both in the church and in society—James's explosive teachings offer us a world of unique possibilities. Let's then hear anew the messages of this practical pastoral theologian.

The Epistle's Purpose and Structure

James is one of the most notoriously difficult New Testament books to outline—and you may have found that to be true when you attempted to outline it (see question 2 on page 17). This becomes even more difficult if you failed to find an organizing theme running through the book. If you found yourself in that position, you are not alone.

Many, including Martin Luther, have not found a focus for the book. It seems to be simply a hodgepodge of ethical exhortations, advice, counsel, and instructions. According to Luther, James just took some sayings from the disciples and threw them down on a piece of paper! It is often felt that he had no specific purpose in mind, that the book's origin had no special occasion. Thus, a survey of commentaries will reveal outlines of the epistle that contain from two to twenty-five major divisions, most of them giving the impression that the epistle is disjointed and lacks a unifying theme.

More and more, however, students of James are coming to realize that the epistle is not a fruit bowl of diverse, unrelated items. Rather, there is a unifying theme around which the letter can be organized. Bible scholars are now recognizing that there is a lens through which the document should be read. I believe that James's theme of suffering is that lens.

The author, as a leader and pastor, was sensitive to the situation of his reading and listening audience. His recipients were living in a collapsing world. They were poor and oppressed. They were persecuted. They were suffering. It is out of this context that James develops a theology of suffering. Let me pause to say here that we must recognize that his concern goes beyond individual suffering.

James is dealing with suffering within the context of communal concern. Peter Davids is correct when he writes that "it is wrong to read the epistle with an individualistic focus. . . . The author addresses the behavior of individuals because that behavior has an impact upon the life of the community" (*James*, 13).

The community of persons to which the epistle is written needs a word of hope, encouragement, and reassurance in its suffering. Oppression, persecution, and other experiences mentioned in the letter should not be seen as the end of existence. Hope will keep these people afloat in their oppressive situations and strengthen them to overcome.

The Epistle's Setting

A careful reading of James demonstrates that much of the context of the suffering it addresses stemmed from social and economic forces and tensions. James seems to have been written at a time when there were severe economic disturbances (5:1-6), social discontent (1:9-11; 2:1-7; 5:4-6), political aggressiveness (4:1-3), and religious upheavals (4:4-12). When we juxtapose this with the fact that the document is very Jewish in its focus (1:1), we conclude that it is an early New Testament work written in Palestine.

The issues of authorship, date, addressees, and life setting are dealt with in depth in commentaries and introductions to the New Testament. (See the suggested readings at the end of this chapter.) I need not engage in extensive discussions on the various arguments here. But it will be helpful for me to state my understanding of these issues in order to place the epistle in its proper context.

Although there are strong arguments for a late date for this letter, the weight of evidence seems to suggest an early date. The presence of a sophisticated Greek and certain problematic phrases (1:1; 5:7, 14) that are used to support the later dating of this epistle may actually indicate later editorial work. This should not surprise us. The Bible is replete with instances in which a later editor (under the inspiration of the Holy Spirit, I believe) added to the original text. Two often cited cases are Deuteronomy 34 (which relates the death of

Moses) and Jeremiah 52. In the latter case it will be noted that Jeremiah 51:64 states "The words of Jeremiah end here." It is obvious, therefore, that chapter 52 is the work of a later editor. In the case of the Epistle of James, it is also possible that an editor or disciple of James could update both the language and theological expressions of James in order to make the document more relevant for a later Christian community or church. I am convinced, however, that the main text and thought of the epistle originated with James, the leader of the group of followers of Jesus mentioned in Acts 15.

It is widely accepted that the Epistle of James is the most Jewish of all the New Testament books. Both its contents and its illustrations are rooted in the Old Testament and in the Jewish documents written during the period between the last Old Testament book and the first century A.D. This Jewishness of the epistle seems to indicate that James wrote his letter very early in the life of the primitive church, probably before the Jerusalem council in A.D. 49 (Acts 15) when Judaism still was part and parcel of even Jesus' followers.

Not only the Jewishness of the document, but also the social conditions it portrays indicate an early date and a composition in Palestine prior to the destruction of Jerusalem in A.D. 70. For example, there are strong hints in chapter 4 of extreme Jewish nationalistic revolutionary activities prior to the full-scale Jewish war with Rome in the late 60s. James is set in this context of violent lawbreaking, murder, and class hatred (4:1-2; 4:6–5:6). These actions and attitudes were characteristics of the Zealots, a nationalistic party or organization in Judaism that sought to overthrow, by violent means, the Roman government and its Sadducean puppets in Jerusalem. It seems to me, therefore, that James is specifically addressing this issue.

The severe socioeconomic situation mentioned in chapters 2 and 5 parallels perfectly the situation in Palestine in the mid-first century. For example, in 2:6 James speaks of the exploitation of the poor by the rich and of the former being dragged into court over the issues of debts, rents, and pledges. In 5:4 the author lashes out at the blatant failure to pay day laborers (farm workers) their wages. These are precisely the types of situations that were endemic to that period of Jewish history in that geographical region.

I will go a step further and propose that James is possibly the earliest New Testament document, written about ten to fifteen years after the resurrection of Jesus. This would date the epistle sometime in the early A.D. 40s. Its content seems to suggest that it was written at a time when there was not a structured, organized Christian community separate from the Jewish community. James possibly still recognized all Jews as God's people and wrote to them as brothers and sisters in the same way Peter spoke to them as brothers and sisters on the day of Pentecost. This presupposition is important to understand if we are to make sense out of many of the troubling features within James. We can note two such troubling features.

In the first place, there is the "controversy" (particularly in the minds of Protestant students of the New Testament, beginning with Luther) regarding the roles of faith and works as presented in Paul's epistles (especially Galatians and Romans) and in James's letter (2:14-26). Who wrote first? Who is attacking whom? Who is correcting whom? For most scholars, James wrote specifically with the intent of correcting Paul. However, as I will attempt to make clear when I deal with 2:14-26, this cannot be the case, since James's concerns are prior to Paul's concern. As a matter of fact, I will demonstrate that their concerns are quite different.

In the second place, there are major Christian theological omissions in the letter—omissions that are unique to James. The only satisfactory answer to these missing fundamental themes is that James wrote his epistle very early, before the Christian church and its leaders (particularly Paul) developed fairly clear and succinct doctrines that distinguished the Christian community of faith from the Jewish non-Christian community. It is to these omissions we must now turn.

The Epistle's Content

Possibly the most glaring omission is the lack of any significant reference to Jesus. The fact is that there are only two direct references (1:1 and 2:1), and neither is intended to make clear Christological points. While James uses the term "Lord" approximately ten times, only in 1:1 and 2:1 is it explicitly clear that the reference is to Jesus.

A strong case can be made that God the Father is the implied subject in each of the other eight instances. As a matter of fact, some would argue that the references to Jesus in 1:1 and 2:1 were inserted by a later Christian editor in order to give James's epistle a clear, unmistakable Christian flavor.

There are other theological issues and doctrines that are explicit in the rest of the New Testament but that are lacking in James. These include the Cross, the Resurrection, the gift and ministry of the Holy Spirit, baptism, the Lord's Supper, worship, and church organization. The lack of these foci indicates to me that the epistle was written at a very early period in the life of Jesus' followers, prior to these issues becoming focal points of discussion and church development.

In addition, it is possible that these omissions are due to the fact that James is reflecting on ethical rather than on doctrinal issues. We must be careful how we make a distinction between ethics and doctrine, especially if we attempt to elevate the latter above the former. The two are interrelated. What one believes and how one lives are equally important. But if we think of doctrine in terms of those categories mentioned above (e.g., the Cross, baptism, etc.) and if we think of ethics in terms of warnings and imperatives, we must admit that James is ethically oriented.

The epistle is possibly the most consistently ethical in the New Testament. In the 108 verses there are approximately sixty imperatives. In no other New Testament book is there a greater frequency of imperatives. As Douglas Moo states, James's purpose "is clearly not so much to inform, but to command, exhort and encourage" (36). Yet, for the most part, his various warnings, precepts, and commands project a tone of pastoral encouragement and exhortation, all intended to give hope to a suffering community.

It is worthwhile to emphasize that James wrote from within what scholars refer to as the tradition of the Jesus movement. That is to say, James was part of the first-century movement within Judaism of which Jesus was the recognized leader—both by His followers as well as by His detractors and opposers. The sources for the activities of this movement, along with their basic practices and beliefs, are found in the Gospels and the Acts of the Apostles. Even though these documents were written decades after Jesus' ministry and the early days of the Jerusalem church, it is widely accepted that they reflect the teachings and activities of Jesus and that of His followers. Since, therefore, James wrote from within that tradition and movement, we should not be surprised that much of his writing parallels the ethical teachings of Jesus found in the Gospels, particularly Matthew and (to a lesser degree) Luke. Of course, even though each of these writers drew on Jesus' teaching, they used them differently and interpreted them differently because their audiences, their settings, and their concerns were different.

James's epistle not only parallels documents that deal with the life, teachings, and general ministry of Jesus but his letter parallels later epistles that address issues in the life of the church late in the first century. The most obvious parallel is with 1 Peter. However, there are many parallels with other Christian writings that did not find their way into our New Testament canon. These include the writings of the Shepherd of Hermas and the epistles of Clement, particularly the first epistle. But in our canonical New Testament, it is 1 Peter that has the closest resemblance to James.

Both James and Peter pursue the topics of trials and submission. But their audiences were different—James's audience was early Jewish; Peter's audience was late Gentile. It is important that as students of Scripture, comparing texts with texts, we not only look for similarities but take note of how the material is used differently in the varied contexts. This can be a model—a paradigm—for how we can appropriate biblical texts for our contemporary scene.

Because James is not developing doctrinal issues, it would be unfruitful to attempt to systematically summarize various theological themes within the epistle. I suspect it will be more useful to ask you to simply join me as I take a brief walk through the letter and take a bird's eye view of the epistle's content.

After James gives traditional greetings to his fellow sufferers "scattered among the nations" (1:1), he tackles the issue that will dominate the letter. The readers are going through trials and suffering—much of it economic (vss. 9-11)—but there is hope. James admonishes them to consider this testing to be joy, for it develops perseverance in this present world (vss. 2-8), and the crown of life will be their ultimate reward (vs. 12). Of course, the trials are not only external; they are also internal, brought on by evil internal desires (vs. 14). These, James makes clear, are not initiated by God (vs. 15). God gives only good and perfect gifts (vss. 17, 18).

Listening is important in the religious development of James's readers. But listening must be followed by active obedience and doing (vss. 19-25). This doing involves more than active outward religious rituals; it includes control of one's tongue and anger (vs. 19) and social activity. This, James emphasizes, is true religion (vs. 27).

The social activity that James is most concerned about is taking care of the oppressed poor; this is the group that seems to be suffering most in his community. The fact is, however, that many of his readers are showing favoritism to the rich at the expense of the suffering poor (2:1-7). For James, whoever favors the oppressive rich over the suffering poor is as much a lawbreaker as is the murderer and adulterer (vss. 8-13; especially vs. 11).

The trials of the poor, hungry, and homeless were also intensified by those who elevated "faith" over "works" (vss. 14-26). It is a pity that we have so often totally missed James's point here by imposing Paul's use of the term "works" upon this passage. For James, "works" is taking care of these economically oppressed persons; for Paul, "works" means a religion of legalistic acts that are meant to bring salvation. Paul, on the one hand, is involved in a theological dispute with Judaizers—those Christians who were demanding that Gentiles who wished to become Christians had to accept and participate in all the legalistic rituals of Judaism, especially circumcision, and become cultural and religious Jews (compare Acts 15:1, 2; Gal. 2:11-16). James, on the other hand, is involved in an ethical confrontation with those who fail to see how their social actions are intensifying the suffering of their fellow human beings. He argues that one is not saved or justified if social works are not combined with faith. This is exactly the point James is making when he writes "What good is it, my brothers, if a man claims to have faith but has no deeds? Can such faith save him? Suppose a brother or sister is without clothes and daily food. If one of you says to him, 'Go, I wish you well; keep warm and well fed,' but does nothing about his physical needs, what good is it? In the same way, faith by itself, if it is not accompanied by action, is dead" (2:14-17). And later James concludes, after giving an illustration in the life and experience of Abraham, "that a person is justified by what he does and not by faith alone" (vs. 24).

James next turns to the issue of wisdom, which his readers need in order to make sense of life's perplexities. Thus James spends an entire chapter on this topic (3:1-18). There is true wisdom and false wisdom. The latter is demonstrated in an inappropriate use of the tongue, which in many instances is at the heart of many trials (vss. 5-9). The former is demonstrated when one performs good deeds (vss. 13, 17), such as those mentioned in chapters 1 and 2 (see 1:27; 2:15).

For the most part, many among the readers of the epistle were not demonstrating true wisdom. Instead, they were involved in fights, quarrels, and slander (4:1-12). It is possible that the stress of suffering brought on, or intensified, this behavior, but it seems that the context is that of the violence instigated prior to the fall of Jerusalem in A.D. 70 by political confrontation between the extreme Jewish nationalists called Zealots, the Romans, and their local political leaders in the Jewish hierarchy. James opposed such behavior. It only exaggerated the suffering.

By now it is clear to the reader that, as far as James is concerned, most of the economic trials his readers are suffering have been caused by the oppressive wealthy. They are the ones who don't care when, where, and how they gain their wealth (vss. 13-17). Nor do they care who suffers because of how they obtain it (5:1-6). James denounces them with the same strong prophetic language used by such Old Testament prophets as Amos and Isaiah. But the denouncement is not so much for the benefit of the wealthy; it was designed to be heard by the poor who were undergoing the trial. It was meant to give them hope. There will be a great reversal; God will bring judgment upon the rich. The great Judge is standing at the door and will bring retribution. The sufferers need only be patient (vss. 7-9). They will receive their reward (see 2:5). Wrongs will be made right in the end.

This letter of hope ends with examples of a patient sufferer whose fortunes were reversed: Job. The same compassion and mercy that was bestowed upon him is available now (5:10-12). James then concludes with the admonition that prayer is a valuable means to alleviate suffering, whether it be sickness or otherwise (vss. 13-20).

Outline of James

I. Trials and Temptations (1:1-18)
   A. Salutation (1:1)
   B. Trials and Endurance (1:1-8)
   C. Poverty and Wealth: The Great Reversal (1:9-11)
   D. Trials and Temptation: Enduring the Test (1:12-18)
II. True Religion (1:19–2:26)
   A. Hearing and Doing (1:19-26)
   B. Caring for the Poor (1:27–2:26)
      1. Acceptance of those who favor the orphans and widows (1:27)
      2. Rejection of those who favor the rich (2:1-13)
      3. Rejection of those who elevate faith above social works (2:14-26)
III. True Wisdom (3:1-18)
   A. Proverbs on the Tongue (3:1-12)
   B. False and True Wisdom (3:13-18)
IV. Disputes, Violence, and Tensions (4:1–5:6)
   A. Violence (4:1-10)
   B. Slander (4:11, 12)
   C. Poverty and Wealth (4:13–5:6)
      1. Tensions brought on by business persons (4:13-17)
      2. Tensions brought on by wealthy farmers (5:1-6)
V. Responses to Suffering (5:7-18)
   A. Patience (5:7-12)
   B. Prayer (5:13-18)
VI. Conclusion (5:19, 20)

For Further Reading

1. For a good treatment on introductory issues relating to James, see Donald Guthrie, *New Testament Introduction*; Ralph P. Martin, *James*; Sophie Laws, *The Epistle of James*; and Peter Davids, *James*.

2. For an extended treatment of my position on date, authorship, and setting, see either Pedrito Maynard-Reid, *Poverty and Wealth in James*, 5-11 or Pedrito Maynard-Reid, "Poor and Rich in the Epistle of James: A Socio-historical and Exegetical Study," 113-132.

3. For an example of how James speaks precisely to a specific culture (in this case, Latin America), see Elsa Tamez, *The Scandalous Message of James*.

4. For a survey and evaluation of the major commentaries, see Ruth B. Edwards, "Which Is the Best Commentary? XV The Epistle of James."

LIST OF WORKS CITED*

Adamson, James B. *James: The Man and His Message*. Grand Rapids, Mich.: Eerdmans, 1989.

Adamson, James B. *The Epistle of James*. The New International Commentary on the New Testament. Grand Rapids, Mich.: Eerdmans, 1976.

Augusburger, David. *Caring Enough to Confront: How to Understand and Express Your Deepest Feelings Toward Others*. Rev. ed. Ventura, Calif.: Regal Books, 1981.

Barclay, William. *The Letters of James and Peter*. Rev. ed. The Daily Study Bible Series. Philadelphia: Westminister, 1976.

Blondel, Jean-Luc. "Theology and Paraenesis in James." *Theology Digest*. 28, no. 3 (1980): 253-256.

Burns, John A. "James, the Wisdom of Jesus." *Criswell Theological Review*, 1, no. 1 (1986): 111-135.

Carlson, Dwight L. *Overcoming Hurts and Anger: How to Identify and Cope With Negative Emotions*. Eugene, Ore.: Harvest House, 1981.

Cedar, Paul A. *James, 1, 2 Peter, Jude*. The Communicator's Commentary. Waco, Tex.: Word, 1984.

Davids, Peter. *Commentary on James: A Commentary on the Greek Text*. New International Greek Testament Commentary. Grand Rapids, Mich.: Eerdmans, 1982.

Davids, Peter H. *James*. New International Biblical Commentary. Peabody, Mass.: Hendrickson, 1989.

Dibelius, Martin. *James*. Rev. by Heinrich Greeven. *Hermeneia* Series. Philadelphia: Fortress, 1976.

Easton, Burton Scott. "The Epistle of James: Introduction and Exegesis." *The Interpreter's Bible*. New York: Abingdon, 1957, 12:3-74.

---

*This list does not include classical works that utilize standard referencing systems across various editions.

Edwards, Ruth B. "Which Is the Best Commentary? XV The Epistle of James." *Expository Times* 103, no. 9 (1992): 263-268.

Elliott, John H. "The Epistle of James in Rhetorical and Social Scientific Perspective: Holiness-Wholeness and Patterns of Replication." *Biblical Theological Bulletin* 23 (Summer 1993): 71-81.

Ellul, Jacques. *Money and Power*. Downers Grove, Ill.: InterVarsity, 1984.

Guthrie, Donald. *New Testament Introduction*. Illinois: InterVarsity, 1973.

Hadidiam, Dikran Y. "Palestinian Pictures in the Epistle of James." *The Expository Times* 63 (1951, 52): 227, 228.

Hartin, Patrick J. " 'Come Now, You Rich, Weep and Wail . . .' (James 5:1-6)." *Journal of Theology for Southern Africa* 84 (September 1993): 57-63.

Hayden, Daniel R. "Calling the Elders to Pray." *Bibliotheca Sacra* 138 (July-September 1981): 258-266.

Hiebert, D. Edmond. "Unifying Theme of the Epistle of James." *Bibliotheca Sacra* 135 (July-September 1978): 221-231.

Howard, Tracy L. "Suffering in James 1:2-12." *Criswell Theological Review* 1, no. 1 (1986): 71-84.

Jeremias, Joachim. "Paul and James." *The Expository Times* 66 (1954, 55): 368-71.

Jeremias, Joachim. *Jerusalem in the Time of Jesus: An Investigation Into Economic and Social Conditions During the New Testament Period*. Philadelphia: Fortress, 1969.

Johanson, Bruce C. "The Definition of 'Pure Religion' in James 1:27 Reconsidered." *The Expository Times* 84 (1972, 73): 118, 119.

Jones, Arthur C. *Wade in the Water: The Wisdom of the Spirituals*. Maryknoll, N.Y.: Orbis, 1993.

Kistemaker, Simon J. *James and I-III John*. New Testament Commentary. Grand Rapids, Mich.: Baker, 1986.

Kistemaker, Simon J. "The Theological Message of James." *Journal of Evangelical Theological Society* 29, no. 1 (March 1986): 55-61.

Kugelman, Richard. *James & Jude*. New Testament Message. Wilmington, Del.: Michael Glazier, 1980.

Laws, Sophie. *The Epistle of James*. Harper New Testament Commentaries. San Francisco: Harper & Row, 1980.

Longenecker, Richard N. "The 'Faith of Abraham' Theme in Paul, James, and Hebrews: A Study in the Circumstantial Nature of New Testament Teaching." *Journal of the Evangelical Theological Society* 20 (1977): 203-212.

Lorenzen, Thorwald. "Faith Without Works Does not Count Before God! James 2:14-26." *The Expository Times* 89 (May 1978): 231-235.

MacArthur, John F., Jr. "Faith According to the Apostle James." *Journal of Evangelical Theological Society* 33, no. 1 (March 1990): 35-41.

Marcus, Joel. "The Evil Inclination in the Epistle of James." *Catholic Biblical Quarterly* 44 (1982): 606-621.

Martin, R. A. *James*. Augsburg Commentary on the New Testament. Minneapolis, Minn.: Augsburg, 1982.

Martin, Ralph P. *James*. Word Biblical Commentary. Waco, Tex.: Word, 1988.

Maynard-Reid, Pedrito U. *Poverty and Wealth in James*. Maryknoll, N.Y.: Orbis, 1987.

Maynard-Reid, Pedrito U. "Called to Share." *Christianity Today* (12 May 1989): 37-39.

Maynard-Reid, Pedrito U. "Poor and Rich in the Epistle of James: A Socio-historical and Exegetical Study." Th.D. dissertation. Berrien Springs, Mich.: Andrews University, 1981.

Mayor, Joseph B. *The Epistle of St. James: The Greek Text With Introduction Notes and Comments*. 2d ed. Grand Rapids, Mich.: Baker, 1978.

McKnight, Scot. "James 2:18a: The Unidentifiable Interlocuter." *Westminster Theological Journal* 52 (1990): 355-364.

Moo, Douglas J. *James*. Tyndale New Testament Commentaries. Grand Rapids, Mich.: Eerdmans, 1985.

Morris, Leon. *Understanding the New Testament: 1 Timothy-James*. Philadelphia: Holman, 1978.

Motyer, Alex. *The Message of James*. The Bible Speaks Today. Downers Grove, Ill.: InterVarsity, 1985.

Neff, David, ed. *The Midas Trap*. Wheaton, Ill.: Christianity Today, 1990.

Nelson, Melvin R. "The Psychology of Spiritual Conflict." *Journal of Psychology and Theology* 4 (Winter 1976): 34-41.

Nichol, Francis D., ed. *Seventh-day Adventist Bible Commentary*. Vol. 7. Washington, D.C.: Review and Herald, 1957.

Poteat, Gordon. "The Epistle of James: Exposition." *The Interpreter's Bible*. New York: Abingdon, 1957, 12:3-74.

Reicke, Bo. *The Epistles of James, Peter, and Jude*. The Anchor Bible. New York: Doubleday, 1964.

Ropes, J. H. *A Critical and Exegetical Commentary on the Epistle of St. James*. The International Critical Commentary. Edinburgh: T & T Clark, 1916.

Schmitt, John J. "You Adulteresses! The Image in James 4:4." *Novum Testamentum* 28, no. 4 (1986): 327-337.

Sidebottom, E. Malcolm. *James, Jude, and 2 Peter*. The Century Bible. Greenwood, S.C: Attic, 1967.

Smit, D. J. "Exegesis and Proclamation: 'Show no partiality . . .' (James 2:1-13)." *Journal of Theology for South Africa* 71 (June 1990): 59-68.

Strauss, Lehman. *James, Your Brother*. Neptune, N.J.: Loizeaux Brothers, 1956.

Stulac, George M. "Who Are 'The Rich' in James?" *Presbyterion: Covenant Seminary Review* 16 (Fall 1990): 89-102.

Stulac, George M. *James*. The IVP New Testament Commentary Series. Downers Grove, Ill.: InterVarsity, 1993.

Tamez, Elsa. *The Scandalous Message of James*. New York: Crossroad, 1992.

Tasker, R. V. G. *The General Epistle of James*. Tyndale New Testament Commentaries. Grand Rapids, Mich.: Eerdmans, 1976.

Townsend, Michael J. "James 4:1-4: A Warning Against Zealotry?" *The Expository Times* 87 (April 1976): 211-213.

Watson, Duane F. "The Rhetoric of James 3:1-12 and a Classical Pattern of Argumentation." *Novum Testamentum* 35, no. 1 (1993): 48-64.

Wells, C. Richard. "The Theology of Prayer in James." *Criswell Theological Review* 1, no. 1 (1986): 85-112.

White, Ellen G. *Counsels to Parents and Teachers*. Boise, Idaho: Pacific

Press Publishing Assn., 1943.

White, Ellen G. *The Desire of Ages*. Boise, Idaho: Pacific Press Publishing Assn., 1940.

White, Ellen G. *The Ministry of Healing*. Boise, Idaho: Pacific Press Publishing Assn., 1942.

White, Ellen G. *Testimonies for the Church*. Boise, Idaho: Pacific Press Publishing Assn, 1948.

White, Ellen G. *Thoughts From the Mount of Blessing*. Boise, Idaho: Pacific Press Publishing Assn., 1956.

Wilkinson, John. "Healing in the Epistle of James." *Scottish Journal of Theology* 24 (1971): 326-345.

Yoder, John. *What Would You Do?* Expanded ed. Scottsdale, Penn.: Herald, 1992.

PART ONE

James 1:1-18

Trials
and
Temptations

CHAPTER ONE

Trials and Endurance

James 1:1-8

> Nobody knows the trouble I see,
> Nobody knows but Jesus.
> Nobody knows the trouble I see,
> Glory, hallelujah!

In recent centuries, few races of people have undergone the pain and suffering that Africans, sold in the slave trade and scattered in the Western Hemisphere, have undergone. Yet, these African slaves in the Caribbean, in South, Central, and North America, after singing "Nobody knows the trouble I see," could say "Glory, hallelujah." These people modeled the exhortations of James in their trials.

Nearly 2,000 years ago, James addressed a community scattered among foreign people (1:1) and undergoing similar intense trials, duress, and sufferings. As an ideal pastor, he recognized their felt needs. He was sensitive to the fact that a letter or sermon dealing with dry, abstract theological and doctrinal issues would not meet their present needs. He would be scratching where it was not itching. Their felt need was how to survive their present suffering. What should they do when trials and temptations overtook them?

In diverse ways throughout this letter, James attempts to be both reactive as well as proactive in dealing with the suffering and trials that faced his community. Here, at the outset of his document, he blends both reaction and proaction. He challenges his readers not only to rejoice in their trials (2:2-4) but also to gain perspective and direction during this period of their existence through the acquisition of wisdom (1:5-8).

■ Getting Into the Word

James 1:1-8

Read James 1:1-8 through two or three times. If possible, read it from two or three different versions. After you have read it a few times, begin to deal with the following questions:

1. If you have access to other translations of the Bible, list in your notebook differences in the translations. In what ways do these differences help you clarify the meaning of the text?
2. What do you think James had in mind when he addressed the recipients of the letter as "the twelve tribes scattered among the nations"? Is the phrase meant to be literal, spiritual, or metaphorical? Explain.
3. Read through the Sermon on the Mount (Matt. 5–7). In columns in your notebook, jot down the texts in Matthew that seem to be saying the same thing as those in James 1:2-8.
4. Use a concordance and/or the marginal references of your Bible and/or a Bible dictionary to identify other biblical texts that speak about the need for wisdom. Does any biblical story come to mind about someone who asked for wisdom? Which story?
5. Why do you think James uses the metaphor of the sea waves to illustrate the doubting person? In what ways does that metaphor help you visualize such a person?
6. Would you say that James views hardship, trials, and sufferings as a realist or an idealist or both? What evidence can you supply from this passage for your answer?

■ Exploring the Word

Salutations

The author of the epistle identifies himself as James (1:1). Apparently, he did not think it essential that he identify himself further, for it may have been obvious to his readers who he was. If, as we suggested in the Introduction, this epistle is one of the earliest New Testament documents, it would seem that the author may have been one of the two Jameses prominent in the early church: James, the son of Zebedee and James, a leader at the Jerusalem Council (Acts 12:17; 15:13; 21:18), who seems to be the same person as the brother of Jesus (Gal. 1:19). James, the son of Zebedee is not recorded as playing a prominent part in the life of the early church. Actually, he was martyred in A.D. 44. In contrast, the other James seemed to be a highly respected figure in the Jerusalem community in the decades of the A.D. 30s and 40s. It seems probable that this latter James is the author of this epistle.

James identifies himself as a servant or slave of God (1:1). Although the Greek term *doulos* (slave, servant) implies absolute loyalty, obedience, and humility, it also can indicate a position of privilege and honor. It is this latter understanding of the term that is prevalent in the Old Testament when the great leaders of Israel are referred to as servants of God. For example, Moses is called "the servant of God" in the postscript to Deuteronomy (34:5). The same use is found in Solomon's majestic prayer when he referred to Moses' leadership in the Exodus (1 Kings 8:53; compare Daniel's prayer in Dan. 9:11) and in God's reference to Moses as "my servant" in the final message of Malachi from the Lord (Mal. 4:4). David is another major figure in Jewish history who is also referred to as servant. In God's words to him (through the prophet Nathan), when God made His great covenant with David and promised him that his (David's) house would be established forever, God called David "my servant" (2 Sam. 7:5, 8; see also Jer. 33:21). And as Ezekiel reiterates God's words regarding the new "covenant of peace" ("the everlasting covenant"), the "servanthood" of David is powerfully invoked (Ezek. 37:24, 25). Prophets in general were also referred to in a few places in the Old Testament as servants who were sent with messages to "stiffnecked people" (Jer. 7:25, 26) and were treated detestably by those people (Jer. 44:4). But it is to those prophets/servants that God always revealed His plans (Amos 3:7). It is in this line of prophets and leaders of God's people that James introduces himself to his readers.

But James also sees himself as a servant of Jesus Christ (1:1). It is possible, as was noted in the Introduction (see p. 17), that this phrase was inserted later under divine guidance by a disciple or Christian editor in order to assure subsequent readers of the epistle's Christian origins and also to reassure them of the author's dedication to the service and lordship of Jesus Christ. Inspiration allows such editorial additions, and they do not take away in the least from the inspired nature of the Word of God. If, however, James himself wrote these words, he is here identifying himself as "a Christian" (a term that was possibly pejoratively given later to Jesus' followers—see Acts 11:26). James would then see himself not only as a Jew standing firmly in the tradition of the Old Testament and its great leaders and prophets but as a follower of his brother Jesus. It should be noted that Paul also calls himself a "servant/slave" but almost always simply as "a servant of Jesus Christ" (Rom. 1:1; Gal. 1:10; Phil. 1:1). Interestingly, Titus 1:1 has "Paul a servant of God and an *apostle of Jesus Christ.*" James, however, is the only New Testament author who uses the dual servanthood combination (servant of God and of Jesus Christ) in his opening address.

James next identifies his audience. His readers are "the twelve tribes scattered among the nations" (1:1). There are two basic views as to who constitute the "twelve tribes." They can either be literal children of Israel—a racial understanding—or the Christian church, a metaphorical understanding.

Those in particular, who believe that James was written late in the first century, or at least after Paul's writings, hold to the metaphorical point of view. In the epistles of Paul and Peter and in Hebrews, the attributes of the nation of Israel are applied to the Christian church. For example, in Romans 9:24-26 the prophets are quoted as predicting the church as the new Israel, and in Galatians Christians are called children of Abraham (3:7-9) and the Israel of God (6:16; compare 1 Pet.2:9, 10; Heb. 3:6). As a matter of fact, throughout the entire book of Hebrews all that pertained to the old religion of Israel now belongs to the Christian church in a superior way. James, then, it is argued, is addressing his epistle to the church—the spiritual "twelve" tribes of Israel.

Other Bible students, however, sense that James is writing to actual Jewish persons and thus take the term "twelve tribes" literally. Some interpreters limit the phrase to Christian Jews; but some, including myself (see *Poverty and Wealth*, 8-11), will argue that James is writing a document that he intends to be heard by both those who are followers of Jesus as well as any other Israelite in his listening community. He is writing to *all* God's people, particularly his fellow, suffering Jewish people. By addressing them as "the twelve tribes," he is simply following a popular way of identifying Jews in those days (Acts 26:7).

We are still left with a problem in this verse. James addresses his readers as "the twelve tribes *scattered among the nations*." In Greek, the word thus translated is *diaspora*. The question that faces us is: Who is the *diaspora*? It is a technical term normally used for Jews living outside Palestine, but it was adopted by Christians later in the first century to highlight their status as strangers and aliens on this earth (1 Pet. 1:1; 1:17; 2:11; Heb. 11:13; 13:14). It is felt by some that James, like the First Epistle of Peter, is using the word in its metaphorical sense. Thus, the recipients are specifically Christian believers—the true Israel—who are scattered throughout the Roman Empire. According to this line of reasoning, most of these have been so scattered because of severe religious persecution. Almost all scholars believe that 1 Peter is addressing a religious persecution situation. The fact is, however, that unlike 1 Peter, there is no evidence of religious persecution in James.

There is another reason why we must understand this word, *diaspora*, differently in James from the way it is used in 1 Peter. In James it has the definite article in the Greek and is thus intended to be used in its absolute sense as referring to the Jewish diaspora, while in 1 Peter it lacks the article and thus should be interpreted in its later technical Christian sense.

It is worthwhile to note that the dispersion of the Jews goes back as early as the ninth century B.C. when Israelites were taken as captives during wars or emigrated for trade purposes (1 Kings 20:34, 35). The first large-scale diaspora, however, was in 722 B.C. when the Assyrians defeated the northern kingdom of Israel, destroyed its capital, Samaria, and carried away into Assyria most of the people belonging to those ten tribes (2 Kings 17:23; 1 Chron. 5:26).

The second large-scale removal of the Israelites happened when Nebuchadnezzar conquered the southern kingdom of Judah, destroyed Jerusalem, and took to Babylon the best and brightest of the population (2 Kings 24:14-16; compare Ps. 137). The third compulsory removal came when the Roman emperor Pompey conquered Jerusalem and the Jews in 63 B.C. and took many of them back to Rome as slaves.

The Jewish Diaspora was not created only by compulsory transplantation due to war. Far greater numbers left Jerusalem and Palestine of their own free wills, as they sought a better life away from home. Two territories in particular then received Jews: Syria to the north and Africa to the south—particularly Alexandria in Egypt, where more than one million Jews lived during the first century A.D.

If James is using the term *diaspora* in this sense, his epistle is then directed to the Jews scattered outside Palestine and not to those persons in the community in which he lives. But the idea that the Diaspora was limited to Jews outside of Palestine may not be correct. There is evidence that Jews of the Diaspora lived in Palestine. As a matter of fact, there were so few Jews in parts of Palestine that they could not be seen as part of the dispersion. Furthermore, Jews of the dispersion were even found in Jerusalem. This seems evident in Acts 2 where it is mentioned that on the day of Pentecost "there were staying in Jerusalem God-fearing Jews from every nation under heaven" (vs. 5). Verses 8-11 go on to list the diverse nationalities representing many language groups, and verse 6 explicitly states that each person heard in his or her own native language. Interestingly, the Jerusalem diasporic Jews even had their own separate communities and their own synagogues, as is evidenced by a synagogue inscription from Jerusalem (see Maynard-Reid, "Poor and Rich," 127).

Although the phrase "scattered among the nations" is used in its absolute sense and thus would normally refer to Jews outside Palestine, it seems to me that James is addressing primarily a community in Palestine (and possibly Syria—for to ancient historians and geographers Palestine and Syria were in reality one unit) with which he was familiar and in which he lived. The passages that address the social situation or depict a social setting indicate that the author is personally engaged with the situation being described. The colors with which he depicts the setting demonstrates that both he and his readers are part of that locale (1:9-11; 2:1-7; 4:1-6, 13-17; 5:1-6).

It is also possible that by addressing his readers as "the diaspora," James is recalling their historical situation. Although many who were scattered abroad went of their free will, the fact remains that much of the dispersion was due to less than ideal circumstances. Dispersion, therefore, was associated with suffering. James's community, scattered among the Gentiles ("nations") of Palestine and undergoing much suffering, would easily grasp the connection and the pun possibly intended by the author.

Turning Defeat Into Victory

James is realistic. He recognized that life is a tale of various trials (1:2). Trials are trials no matter what form they take. They may be many-colored and variegated, diverse, complex, and intricate. They may be simple and a passing irritation, but they are trials nonetheless. None of us enjoy trials. Our ideal state is one of happiness, ease, comfort, and ultimate security—pleasurable undisturbed tranquility! But James knows that that is not reality. We all face trials daily.

In the New Testament, the word translated "trials" is *peirasmos*. It is the same word translated "temptation." Only the context can determine whether it means external affliction (trials) or the inner enticement to sin (temptation). James deals with both meanings at the beginning of the letter. The inward desire, temptation, is dealt with in verses 13-15. But here in these very opening verses of the chapter, James deals with trials of many kinds, those that encompass the range of hardships that are common to all people. In James's community, these included social and economic adversities (1:27; 2:1-6; 5:4), illnesses (5:14-16), and interpersonal tensions (4:1-12). Today, suffering includes the daily pressures of job, marriage, family burdens, serious illness, financial crises, persecution—religious and social—

and any tragic experience. It can be anything that brings tears, pain, and sweat.

For all of us James has an idealistic solution that is quite realistic. First, he says: Consider it pure joy (1:2)! There is a warmth in his tone toward those he addresses as brothers and sisters. It indicates the spirit of fellowship and oneness that he feels with his readers. It is only because he understands their experience that he can exhort them to consider it *pure* (all, full, supreme nothing but, unmixed) joy whenever they faced trials of many kinds. Only as we experience the pain of others, only as we are incarnated into their suffering, can we encourage them to rejoice.

Now, James is not saying that we should seek for trouble and court disaster in order to be happy. He is not here supporting the person who fosters a martyr complex or the unrealistic person who finds absolute good in everything—a kind of pollyanish person. He is not arguing that we must derive unnatural satisfaction from suffering. Normal people do not enjoy trials. In fact, we do everything to avoid trials. But James is writing to people who, through no fault of their own, are undergoing trials. To them he does *not* say "trial *is* pure joy." Rather, he tells them to look on the bright side and turn their suffering into the highest good—"*consider* it pure joy" (vs. 2).

Jesus spoke in a similar manner in His Sermon on the Mount when he said: "Blessed are you when people insult you, persecute you and falsely say all kinds of evil against you because of me. Rejoice and be glad, because great is your reward in heaven, for in the same way they persecuted the prophets who were before you" (Matt. 5:11, 12).

Turning defeat into victory by considering it pure joy when one faces trials is a paradox that many who have no relationship with Jesus fail to understand. But Paul understood it when he wrote: "We are hard pressed on every side, but not crushed; perplexed, but not in despair, persecuted, but not abandoned; struck down, but not destroyed. We always carry around in our body the death of Jesus, so that the life of Jesus may also be revealed in our body" (2 Cor. 4:8-10).

Tests and trials, sorrows and disappointments, are opportunities for growth and development. As William Barclay said, "They are not meant to make us fall; they are meant to make us soar. They are not meant to defeat us; they are meant to be defeated. They are not meant to make us weaker; they are meant to make us strong" (43). When James says that the testing of faith develops perseverance (1:3), he is not saying that trials determine whether a person has faith or not. What he is indicating is that trials strengthen the faith (not intellectual assent as some interpret faith in 2:19, but trust, as in 2:1) that is already present.

The perseverance or steadfastness that results or is accomplished through the testing and trials has traditionally been understood as patience, i.e., a passive, submissive attitude. But the word James uses here has an active sense. This is demonstrated in the perseverance of Job referred to in 5:11. In the extratestamental book 4 Maccabees, the same word is used to describe the courage and endurance of the mother of the heroes—her sons and Eleazar—who ultimately were instrumental in defeating the Syrian aggressors and oppressors.

The fourth book of Maccabees does not appear in our Protestant English canon, but it is an appendix to the Greek translation of the Old Testament—the Septuagint, or LXX. For our purposes here, it is important to note that the word James uses for "perseverance" (hupomonē) occurs more often in this book than any other book in the LXX. The story of the mother, her sons, and Eleazar illustrates the word's meaning. The incident is set in the second century B.C. when the Syrian (or Seleucid) tyrant Antiochus IV Epiphanes ruled Jerusalem. In his determination to destroy Judaism and replace it with Greek culture (Hellenism), he banned the reading of the Old Testament, Sabbath keeping, and circumcision. He even went as far as offering a pig upon the main altar of the temple! These measures were resisted by a number of Jews who, as a result, met with death at the hand of this brutal ruler. Fourth Maccabees tells stories of the torture and martyrdom of the elder priest Eleazar (5:1–7:23), of the seven brothers (8:1–14:10), and of their mother (14:11–18:19). In these descriptions of suffering and death, the author praises the courage, endurance, and opposition to the tyrannical king of these martyrs, which was seen as precipitous in bringing about the defeat of

Antiochus. He writes: "By their endurance they conquered the tyrant, and thus their native land was purified through them" (4 Macc. 1:11, NRSV).

James, then, seems to be calling for a kind of militant, heroic patience and perseverance like that in 4 Maccabees. It is a call to be immovable, unbreakable, and constant. There seems to be, implicit in the term, a call to resist trials and overcome them. James challenges his readers not to succumb to pain and oppression. It is this challenging response that brings the pure joy referred to in James 1:2.

This active perseverance brings one to the level of maturity and completion (vs. 4). The word translated "maturity" in the NIV is traditionally "perfect." James likes the word *perfect*. It is a key term for him. In no other New Testament book is it used as much as in James. But James is not speaking here of sinless perfection. He is not referring to the overt absence of any sin in a person's life. The word for James has reference to maturity as the NIV rightly translates it. The concept is primarily about a mature person's character—a character that demonstrates love. This then would be similar to the perfection that Jesus called for in Matthew 5:48. In the context of the Sermon on the Mount, to be perfect as God is perfect is to love everyone, including one's enemies (Matt. 5:43-48).

When perseverance has made us mature and complete with a wholeness of fellowship with God and our fellow human beings, we have reason to rejoice—reason for pure joy. We can say with Paul, "We also rejoice in our sufferings, because we know that suffering produces perseverance; perseverance, character; and character, hope. And hope does not disappoint us, because God has poured out his love into our hearts by the Holy Spirit, whom he has given us" (Rom. 5:3-5).

Losing Perspective and Direction

Persons who are going through trials do not normally find it natural to rejoice; instead, there is the tendency to lose perspective and direction. For James the solution to this problem is the acquisition of wisdom (1:5). This wisdom, of course, is not some modern philosophic speculation or dry intellectual erudition. James was possibly well acquainted with the Greek understanding of wisdom, which is close to modern philosophic speculation. The Stoics, for example, defined wisdom as the *knowledge* of divine and human things; for them, wisdom was a "science." For James, on the other hand, like the early Hebrew people, wisdom was not speculative, but practical. James thinks like the wisdom writers (the sages) before him, who saw wisdom as concerned with the business of life. This is the sense given by the first proverb in the most extensive wisdom book of the Old Testament: "For attaining wisdom and discipline; for understanding words of insight; for acquiring a disciplined and prudent life, *doing what is right and just and fair*" (Prov. 1:2, 3. Compare Proverbs 2, 3, which deal with the moral benefits of wisdom). This wisdom, as far as the ancient sages were concerned, comes only from God: "For the Lord gives wisdom, and from his mouth come knowledge and understanding" (2:6). James is clearly thinking in Jewish, not in Greek, categories. For him, wisdom is a practical thing that only God can give. Thus James encourages us to ask God for wisdom—and ask continually. The Greek grammar indicates that the request for wisdom must not be a one-time action. It is continuous action.

Our author is here echoing the teaching of Jesus in Matthew 7:7-11 and Luke 11:9-13 where the hearer is admonished to ask and it will be given. However, instead of Matthew's "good gifts" and Luke's "Holy Spirit," James suggests that the reader ask for the gift of wisdom. When a person asks for wisdom, he or she should remember two things: (1) how God gives; He gives generously without finding fault (1:5), and (2) how the one asking should ask; he should ask without doubts (vs. 6).

God's giving is unwavering, unreserved, and uncalculating. The word translated "generously" is found only in this text in the New Testament, but it carries the meaning of "without mental reservation." God, therefore, is absolutely willing to give—without hesitation, sincerely and without mental reservation. He does not grumble and complain. He does not criticize and find fault. He never rebukes us for asking too much. He never reproaches and reprimands when we ask. God's commitment is total and unreserved.

Part two of the equation is that we must believe and not doubt. James now turns from the manner in which God gives to the manner in which we are to ask. The way in which God meets our request is limited by the manner in which we ask. Although God has no mental reservation, there is a condition attached to the promise. The petitioner must ask in faith without doubting (vs. 6). Jesus' saying in Matthew 21:21, 22 is apropos: " 'I tell you the truth, if you have faith and do not doubt . . . you can say to this mountain, "Go, throw yourself into the sea," and it will be done. If you believe, you will receive whatever you ask in prayer.' "

In this passage, the nature of the doubt we are warned about is not absolutely clear. Whether it is doubt about the object of request or what is really desired or the outcome of the request is not the main point. The fact that God is willing and able to give the wisdom that He has promised is what the text is driving at.

The person who doubts is one who is strongly influenced by adversity and diverse circumstances. That person is unstable and is as shifting as the unsettled behavior of the waves, which, under the influence of the varied winds, are driven in one direction and soon after in another. Such an individual is double-minded and unstable (1:6-8).

This double-mindedness is the opposite of the maturity, completeness, and perfection mentioned in verse 4. James most likely coined the word *double-minded*, which literally means "two-souled" or "double-spirited." Since the Hebrew people accepted the fact that the "soul" equals one's entire self, one's whole person (e.g., Gen. 2:7), a double-souled person, then, for James, would be a sort of Siamese twin, each looking in opposite directions. John Bunyan in *Pilgrim's Progress* dubbed such a person "Mr. Facing-both-ways."

In the Sermon on the Mount, Jesus spoke about a person who attempts to be double-minded when he declared that "no one can serve two masters. Either he will hate the one and love the other, or he will be devoted to the one and despise the other. You cannot serve both God and Money" (Matt. 6:24). In reality, such a person's devotion is not on God but on something other than God—whether it be on self, materialism, or some other influence.

It is interesting that James suggests that double-minded persons are not merely unstable in what we would call spiritual things. They are unstable in all areas of life ("in all he does," 1:8)—in their everyday affairs with others, in their actions, habits, and thoughts—during their journey through life. If we are to endure the trials that afflict us daily and consider them pure joy, we cannot afford to lose perspective and direction in any area of our lives. The only solution is to obtain the heavenly wisdom that God is anxious to give (vs. 5).

■ Applying the Word

James 1:2-8

1. How would I tell a family member or a friend who is blind, paralyzed, sick with an incurable disease, sexually or physically abused, etc., to consider his or her trial and suffering to be pure joy? Are there times when it is better not to say anything? Explain.
2. When I meet frustrations, difficulties, crises, and adversities, do I become cynical, skeptical, depressed, angry, etc.? Or do I shout, "Praise the Lord"? Or do I have other methods of coping? Explain.
3. Does God always grant me my needs without hesitation or mental reservation? If I do not receive, am I always at fault, or are there other reasons? If you feel that other reasons may be involved, list them.
4. Is doubting always sinful? If *Yes*, how do I explain the natural questionings that are part of human nature? If *No*, doesn't my answer contradict James? Explain the reasons for your answer.
5. In what specific ways do I see myself as a double-minded person? What areas in my life need more stability?

■ Researching the Word

1. Using a Bible dictionary and/or a Bible encyclopedia, look up the word *dispersion* or *diaspora*. List two or three points about how the Jewish dispersion ultimately aided the spread of the Christian gospel.

2. Use a comprehensive concordance to discover the various ways the Greek word translated "trial" and "temptation" (*peirasmos*) is used. List those instances in which the translation would be clearer if the other English word would have been used. Explain your reasoning for each case. Summarize your conclusions on the New Testament's use of these two words. Compare your findings with the conclusions in a Bible dictionary or encyclopedia.

3. Look up the word *perfect* in a concordance based on the King James Version. Select randomly ten passages in the New Testament in which it is used. Can you identify any in which it is absolutely clear that the context is dealing with sinless perfection? Explain. What other synonyms would you use in each case? Compare several different translations of verses that use the word. List the synonyms you find there. Then read the article on perfection in a Bible dictionary.

■ Further Study of the Word

1. For an excellent article that treats the subject matter of this chapter, see T. L. Howard, "Suffering in James 1:2-12."

2. For a study of a specific group of people who have been able to find joy in trials through the medium of song, see A. C. Jones, *Wade in the Water: The Wisdom of the Spiritual*. See especially the second chapter, "Sometimes I Feel Like a Motherless Child: Suffering and Transformation" (18-38).

3. For a fairly technical article that shows how a faith-doubt conflict corresponds to the typical approach-avoidance and approach-approach paradigms in psychology, see M. Nelson, "Psychology of Spiritual Conflict."

4. For a fine commentary on the Christian and suffering, see E. G. White's chapter "Help in Daily Living," 469-482 of *The Ministry of Healing*; especially the section entitled "The Discipline of Trial" (470-472).

CHAPTER TWO

Upside Down

James 1:9-11

James 1:9-11 has been one of the most troublesome passages of Scripture from the time it was penned by its author. Not because it is difficult to understand, but because it goes against society's norms and values. Initially, it must have been difficult for the rich hearers and readers in James's community to be sarcastically denounced so early in the letter. It is quite possible that their reaction was one of dismissal and rejection of the writer's comments.

By the second and third centuries when the epistle began to gain wider circulation, it had a hard time being accepted as part of the canon. It has been suggested that this was due in part to verses such as 1:9-11, that offended the growing number of wealthy persons who began to join the Christian church. James, thus, was one of the last books to be canonized—nearly 300 years after it was written.

In recent centuries, with the dominance of capitalism and free-market economies in predominantly Christian nations, these verses in James are not seen as appropriate sermonic or Bible study material. They seem to go against the Great Dream—the American, the Jamaican, the Brazilian, the Haitian Dream! They go against the theological assumption that if you serve God and pay your tithe and offerings you will be wealthy, while poverty is a sign of God's displeasure and His curse.

Is it possible to put behind us the centuries of understanding and misunderstanding of the text and hear James rigorously in his context? Is it possible even to temporarily bury our economic and political ideology and hear God's Word afresh, no matter how difficult that may be?

■ Getting Into the Word

James 1:9-11

Read verses 9-11 two or three times. Meditate on them. Pray. Ask God for wisdom to grasp and accept His word; then respond to the following:

1. Read carefully 1:9-11; 2:1-8; 4:13-16; 5:1-6. List in your notebook the characteristics of the poor; then list the characteristics of the rich. Do you find any verse(s) that clearly characterize these concepts as spiritual rather than economic? If so, state which ones. Explain why you interpret it/them spiritually. If not, explain why these verses should be interpreted only in an economic manner.
2. Read 1:9-11. Then read verses 2-8. In what ways do verses 9-11 directly relate to the earlier verses? List these in your notebook.
3. Compare verses 9-11 with the parable of the Rich Man and Lazarus (Luke 16:19-31). List all the similarities you discover. Can you find other passages in Luke that parallel these verses? List them.

■ Exploring the Word

Poor but Rich

In the previous chapter I attempted to show that James exhorted his readers to consider it pure joy when they faced all kinds of trials (1:2). In verses 9-11 we find the first example of the intense trials being faced by people within his community.

The person in humble circumstances (vs. 9), the poor individual, is the one who is possibly meeting the most severe trials. Why else would James make this his first illustration? And why else would he deal with this issue more extensively than any other in his small document?

James is concerned here with giving hope and encouragement to the suffering poor within his community. He not only encourages these persons in humble circumstances, who are meeting trials of many kinds, to actively persevere (vs. 3) but he also tells them that they must be steadfast in their exaltation—they must take pride in their "high position" (vs. 9). These are positive words of hope for a hurting people.

If, as we just now suggested, the poor, humble person of verse 9 is one of the persons undergoing trials in verse 2, then we are looking at a parallel between the first and second major paragraphs of this letter. I would suggest, then, that verses 9-11 stand parallel with, and as an illustration of, the introductory overview given in verses 2-9. This becomes even more clear if we can draw a parallel between the double-minded person in verse 8 with the rich person in verses 10 and 11. This is possible when we recognize (as was mentioned in the previous chapter of this commentary) that one of the marks of a double-minded person is the attempt to serve both God and money (see Matt. 6:24). If this was what James had in mind, then not only is the poor, "humble" person (1:9) the steadfast person of verses 2 and 3 but the rich, proud person (vss. 10, 11) is the double-minded, wavering individual of verses 6-8.

The word translated "humble circumstances" in verse 9 literally means "low, flat, mean, insignificant, weak, poor." It refers to the oppressed and afflicted. As in Luke 1:52, the reference is to economic poverty in contrast to wealth. This person is low on the socio-economic ladder and is powerless. It is important to note that the many biblical words for "poor" have both physical as well as spiritual connotations, i.e., external as well as internal references. There is the outward condition of poverty and oppression as well as the inner spiritual condition with reference to one's character.

Many have used this spiritual understanding to take the bite out of James's message. They view the person in humble circumstances, or the poor, as "the poor in spirit" of Matthew 5:3. Such "poor," it is argued, are those who have a relationship with God. There are a number of references in the Old Testament and particularly in the intertestamental literature in which the term *poor* can be understood metaphorically and spiritually (for example, Ps. 86:1; Dubelius,

39-45). In these cases the "poor" are the pious who trust in God and are His devotees. No consideration is given in such passages to whether the "poor" are economically wealthy or destitute. It is very possible, even more than likely, that the economically poor in James's community are simultaneously lacking in material possessions, yet pious, devoted to God and spiritually poor. But a careful reading of the epistle amply demonstrates that James is not at all emphasizing the spiritual, internal aspect of poverty; rather, he is laying stress on the social and economic situation of the poor (2:6; 5:1-5).

James encourages the poor to take pride in their "high position" (1:9). This phrase can be translated as "boast in their exaltation." The command to take pride, to boast, to glory, resembles the exhortation in verse 2 to consider it joy when they faced trials. The pride and boasting in this context is not one of arrogant self-importance. Conversely, it is, in part, as Douglas Moo writes, "the joyous pride possessed by the person who values what God values" (67).

We have to concede that most of us have found it easier to rejoice when wealth comes than when it goes, when we have it than when we don't. Most of us complain if we can't get ahead. James recognized the difficulty of poverty. There is no question in his mind it is a trial; it is at the root of the suffering of his community. But he still encourages the poor. They may be poor but they are rich. They have a high position. Their riches and high position are not in the realm of economic possession and social position; rather, it is in terms of their status with God. They are God's chosen people and His special possession (2:5). They are exalted in the present reign of God and possess the kingdom of God (vs. 5; compare Luke 1:52, 53; 6:20) while awaiting the future reign of God. They become possessors of the spiritual and material rewards of the heavenly inheritance. The poor have, therefore, the real exaltation, which only God can give. For this they can rejoice.

Rich but Poor

Although James is particularly interested in the suffering of the poor, it is the rich who occupy the majority of his attention throughout the epistle (2:1-7; 4:13-17; 5:1-6). His great emphasis is on their downfall (1:10, 11; 4:14; 5:1-3). It is clear that he is doing this in order to draw the precise contrast between the outcome of the poor and that of the rich.

As noted earlier, James's explicit position vis-a-vis the rich is hard for many to accept. Many, instead of reading the epistle rigorously, create interpretations in order to placate the wealthy Christians within our contemporary communities. But we need to read the difficult texts within their difficult contexts and allow them to speak for themselves without imposing our concerns upon them.

One of the problems that perennially arises in this passage is whether the rich person is a Christian church brother or not. Some say he is not; therefore, the text is not applicable to church members. Others argue that the wealthy person is a church member whose wealth will be lost through the trials referred to in 1:2. What such interpreters fail to realize (or simply ignore) is that it is not the riches that will pass away but the rich person (vs. 10).

The issue is not whether the rich is a church member or not. This has no relevance in this context. As a matter of fact, James is not even dealing with the rich as a class or the rich as an individual. These are not the issues here. He is simply contrasting poor and rich. The former can truly boast because there is exaltation. The latter will be brought low and fade away. James is working with the theme of exaltation-humiliation turned upside down. In this scheme he gives hope to the poor by letting them realize that even though they seem humiliated and down, they really are exalted and up. God, in turning everything upside down, brings down the rich and humiliates them.

When one reads this passage, as well as 2:5-7 and 5:1-6, it seems that James does not approve of any rich person at all. His threat to them is unqualified by any consideration that there might be a righteous wealthy person. Whenever he speaks about the rich, his words and tone are always negative. His language lacks any semblance of hope for them.

Whenever I treat this, or similar passages, in my classes or in a church setting, the question invariably arises: How could James speak like that? Didn't he know rich persons such as Nicodemus, Joseph of Arimathea, Mary of Bethany, and Barnabas? But the answer to the first question is: Were any of these people really rich at the time of James's writing? Hadn't they shared all their wealth and become part of the suffering community in Jerusalem (Acts 2:42-47; 4:32-37)? If that be the case, it becomes clear why James had no good word for the rich. In effect, those who had failed to share their wealth would actually be outside the community.

To make his point quite forceful, James draws on Isaiah 40:6-8 for his imagery: "All men are like grass, and their glory is like the flower of the field. The grass withers and the flowers fall, because the breath of the Lord blows on them. Surely the people are grass. The grass withers and the flowers fall, but the word of our God stands forever." James, however, does not end on a word of hope as Isaiah does. He develops a striking judgmental punch line.

James takes this illustration from nature (which was familiar not only to himself and Isaiah but to all who lived in Palestine) to describe the sure fate not of *all* people but of the rich only. He uses the image of flowers and of green herbage—good images of transitoriness. The picture is that of a brief but brilliant Palestinian spring—a phenomenon that continues even to the present. Flowers like the anemone, cyclone, and lily bloom profusely but are gone within weeks in Palestine.

Our author then draws on another phenomenon that is almost unique to Palestine. He speaks of the sun *and* the scorching heat (1:11). (Note, I believe the translation "and" rather than "with" does better justice to what James is portraying.) The focus is on the sun as a destructive agent, and the heat—the sirocco—is the blasting, scorching southeast wind of the desert, which blows incessantly night and day during the spring. This heat can change the color of the landscape from green to brown in a single day and is fatal to young growth and flowers. James likens the rich to these flowers, which seemingly are powerful, strong, majestic, and beautiful, yet in the height of their glory are cut down suddenly, abruptly, and completely.

Again, we must emphasize that the issue here is not one of wealth. It is not wealth that will pass away. It is the wealthy upon whom the judgment comes (vs. 10). James does not seem to have a problem with wealth per se (an argument from silence, I grant). His problem is with the rich who, it would seem, are the ones who are bringing trials and suffering upon the poor. This will be made clearer in chapters 2 and 5 of the epistle. The judgment upon them will come as they engage in their business pursuits, as they participate in their commercial travel and enterprises. This is the issue addressed in 4:13-17.

For James, it is clear the rich are, or will be, turned upside down. In the area of confidence and security, things are surprisingly reversed. The poor are also turned upside down. From humble circumstances and poverty they receive a high position. These are wonderfully encouraging words for persons who are undergoing severe economic trials. They are assured that a great reversal will take place. The suffering poor, whose poverty has come about as a result of oppression by the rich of the first century (as James makes clear in 2:6 and 5:1-6), now can rejoice because God is turning, and will turn, things upside down.

Although James seems to stand out in the New Testament in his strident view of the wealthy, the fact is that he is not alone in his proclamation. Of the four Gospels, Luke is particularly explicit in this exaltation-humiliation motif. Very early in his Gospel, Luke relates the promise of God to exalt the poor and to judge the powerful and rich. This is voiced by Mary in her song (Luke 1:46-55), traditionally known as the Magnificat: "He has brought down rulers from their thrones but has lifted up the humble. He has filled the hungry with good things but has sent the rich away empty" (vss. 52, 53). This is also true in Luke's version of the Sermon on the Mount, which he presents as a Sermon on a Level Place (6:17-49). Unlike Matthew, who has "Blessed are the poor in spirit" (5:3), Luke simply has "Blessed are you poor" (6:20). And Luke has the reversal line that Matthew lacks but that parallels James's thoughts: "But woe to you rich, for you have already received your comfort" (vs. 24).

Luke's Gospel is laced through and through with this upside-down theme. He, like James, walks in the footsteps of such eighth-century B.C. prophets as Amos, Micah, and Isaiah, who demonstrated God's special care and concern for the poor and the damnation of the oppressive rich (Amos 2:6-8; 4:1-3; 5:11-13; Mic. 6:6-16; Isa. 1:10-26). Luke consistently has Jesus telling stories in which the wealthy succumb to the ultimate judgment—e.g., The Rich Fool (Luke 12:13-21) and the Rich Man and Lazarus (16:19-31). In Luke, Jesus is also involved in incidents in which it is clear that the rich cannot have salvation unless they share their wealth with the poor and oppressed—e.g., The Rich Ruler (18:18-30) and Zacchaeus (19:1-10).

James, Jesus, and Luke would clearly have problems in today's society. We today have our values reversed from that of the New Testament. Jacques Ellul in *Money and Power* has demonstrated that in our present economic system money functions as the measuring rod of values. The rich, then, are the ones to be emulated. People are measured by what they possess. Those who have it are praised and extolled. Those who don't are pitied and denigrated. The poor are viewed as being cursed by God; the rich are considered as being exalted by God.

I'm not attempting to draw exact parallels between our twentieth-century world and the oppressive economic situation in first-century Palestine. But the fact is, as we will see later, there are parallels. And if we are to be true to James and to our Lord Jesus Christ, we, too, must give hope to the oppressed poor, while at the same time challenging the oppressive rich who refuse to share with those in humble circumstances.

■ Applying the Word

James 1:9-11

1. If I find myself to be wealthy in comparison to those around me, how should I understand James's words in these verses? What do they say to me? What should I do about his message?
2. What if your pastor should preach on verses 9-11 without balancing it out by saying, "It does not mean that all rich persons will be lost or 'fade away' "? How would you feel?

Do you think that James would be more effective if he gave such a "balancing" statement? Explain your answer.

3. Besides poor and rich, are there other categories or contrasts in contemporary life to which James's concern can apply? In what other areas could you see a great reversal—an upside down—taking place? Be specific.

4. Draw two column in your James notebook. At the top of one write "Positive Pride" at the top of the other write "Negative Pride." List in the first column actions, lifestyle, or relationships in which you can genuinely boast—positively. In the next column, list those actions, lifestyle, and relationships with which you could be ashamed. Did you find some that could go either way? Which were they? Why?

■ Researching the Word

1. In your concordance look up the word *poor*. Choose ten passages from the minor prophets (Hosea to Malachi) that contain this word and read them and their immediate context. List the similarities you find with James. Do the same for the word *rich* and/or *wealthy*. Now look under the Gospel of Luke and find five texts for each category and repeat the exercise.

2. Utilize a concordance to find all the references in which the Bible writers liken human life to a flower. List the various lessons that can be gleaned from such a study. Compare your findings with the discussion of "flower" in a Bible dictionary.

■ Further Study of the Word

1. For an excellent commentary that is detailed and sensitive to the social setting of this passage, see R. P. Martin, *James*.

2. See P. Maynard-Reid, *Poverty and Wealth in James* for a detailed study of this passage. Especially see the chapter "The Great Reversal," 38-47.

3. For a biblical exposition on how the Christians are called to share their wealth with the poor, see P. Maynard-Reid, "Called to Share" in *The Midas Trap* (65-70), ed. David Neff. The entire book, many chapters of which originally appeared in *Christianity Today* (12 May 1989), is an excellent resource for an evangelical perspective on the issue of poverty and wealth. See also G. M. Stulas, "Who Are 'the Rich' in James?"

4. E. G. White has numerous statements that speak to the issue of sharing with the poor. An extended piece on this is found in *Testimonies for the Church*, 3:511-521, entitled "Duty to the Unfortunate."

CHAPTER THREE

Blessing
or Blaming

James 1:12-18

When an individual meets with trials, losses, setbacks, injustices, and suffering, how should he or she respond? This is the question that now preoccupies James. He suggests there are two responses—one positive and the other negative. He already outlined the positive when he told his readers to consider it pure joy whenever they faced many kinds of trials (1:2). The reason for such positive thinking is because such trials develop perseverance (vs. 3). James continues with this line of reasoning when he attempts to answer his implied question: "How does one respond to trials, losses, setbacks, injustices, and sufferings?" The first answer is, positively—with perseverance (vs. 12).

But there is also a negative response to sufferings and trials. Within James's community there were those who, rather than persevering and considering it pure joy when they faced difficulties (vss. 2, 3, 12), not only succumbed to the effects of the trials but blamed God for tempting them. In their minds, God became the source and first cause of such evil. James reacts by offering a kind of practical theodicy—an explanation of the existence of evil in light of the goodness and sovereignty of God. It is not God who tempts; rather, such temptation results from an inner, personal, evil desire. For James, God does not lead into temptation (compare Matthew 6:13; Luke 11:2); He is not the originator of evil and temptation; He is the source of only good things. He gives only good and perfect gifts (1:16-18).

■ Getting Into the Word

James 1:12-18

After reading verses 12-18 a couple of times, do the following exercises:

1. Look up the texts listed in the margins or footnotes of your Bible. Jot down those texts appearing elsewhere in the Bible with the most striking analogies to this passage in James. Did you find any texts that differed with James or that enhanced your understanding of James's argument? Which ones were they? If you found differences, how do you explain them?
2. Read verses 12-15. Do you find instances where it would be better or more natural to use the word *trial* instead of *temptation*, and vice versa? Write out your own paraphrase of these verses using *trial* or *temptation* where it seems more appropriate. State in parentheses why you made these choices.
3. Look up the words *temptation, tempt,* or any derivative of them in a Bible concordance. List those passages that indicate who or what is the source of temptation. Compare these texts with James's argument in verses 13-15. Explain James's contention as to the source of temptation in light of the passages you found.
4. Use a concordance to identify texts that speak about a "crown" as a gift or a reward. List those texts. Beside each passage make a notation whether (according to the context) the reference is to a victor's crown (athletic or military) or a royal crown.

■ Exploring the Word

Blessings From Perseverance

The theme of suffering continues to preoccupy the mind of James in 1:12-18. He is working with a single thought at the beginning of his epistle (vss. 2-18). His focus is on the trials that his community is undergoing. Earlier we noted that the sufferings, the trials, are varied and of many kinds (vs. 2). Although James doesn't give examples of those trials in verses 2-8, a reading of the rest of the epistle seems to confirm that his concern is mainly with external trials. His focus is on such distress and ordeals as, for example, economic oppression (2:6; 5:4), physical fights (4:1, 2), sickness (5:14), and other types of trouble (vs. 13). It is clear from his first illustration in 1:9-11 that he wishes his readers to understand that the trials he is dealing with are external. In verses 9-11 he outlines, in no uncertain terms, the Great Reversal: The rich, who are doing well and are clearly not facing any trials, will pass away and be destroyed (vss. 10, 11). On the other hand, the poor, who are in humble circumstances and are facing the trial of economic subsistence, will be exalted (vs. 9).

It is in this line of thought that James offers his first of two beatitudes (vs. 12; see vs. 25 for the other). The blessing is upon those who have a positive response when facing trials. It is worthwhile to note here that verse 12 is a pivotal verse in James's structure and argument. It is part of an argument as to how the sufferer responds to trials. The response can be either positive or negative. The sufferer can respond by persevering (vs. 12) or by blaming God, accusing Him of tempting the sufferer (vs. 13). We noted earlier that both words—*trials* and *temptations*—are translations of the same Greek word, *peirasmos*. "Trials" refer to external suffering, while "temptation" has reference to inner testing. It seems fairly clear that in vs. 2 James is speaking about the external pressures that one undergoes daily. In verses 13 and 14, however, *peirasmos* seems to denote the internal experience of temptation to commit sin. Our question here is: What is its meaning in verse 12? Most scholars interpret *peirasmos* here in the same way as in verse 2, arguing that 1:12 is either concluding the argument of all the verses preceding it or simply reverting back to, and paralleling, verse 2. Other Bible students interpret *peirasmos* in verse 12 differently. Rather than a concluding verse to verses 1-11, verse 12 is perceived as an introductory verse to 13-15, and, therefore, should be translated "temptation." It seems, however, that in verse 12 James is aware of the ambiguity of the word and is playing upon its double meaning. This verse serves, then, as a transition verse; it summarizes the argument of verses 2-11 and at the same time introduces the discussion in verses 13-18. The fact is, both external trials and internal temptations are parts of the perennial struggles we face in our day-to-day existence.

The positive response to trials in James is perseverance. James here (vs. 12) repeats the position he stated in verses 2-4. When we face trials of any kind (oppression, injustice, an attack, a setback, a loss, sickness, etc.), we should consider it pure joy and persevere. In verse 12 he continues to extol the virtues of endurance and perseverance by employing the same vocabulary he used earlier. The perseverance in both places is an active one. It involves resistance and courage, not the passive, submissive attitude that we sometimes call "patient endurance." As we noted in our exploration of verses 2-4, James's use of perseverance has an active sense in this context. It is the same word as that used in the extratestamental book, 4 Maccabees, for the aggressive courage and endurance of the seven brothers, their mother, and the priest Eleazar who were instrumental in the defeat of the Syrian oppressors in the second century B.C. (see chapter 1, page 47). Perseverance, therefore, has the meaning of active resistance. It further refers to one who is constant, irremovable, and unbreakable—a person who will not succumb to pain, oppression, distress, and despair. Such a person is promised a blessing.

This verse (vs. 12) is reminiscent of Jesus' eighth and ninth beatitudes in Matthew's version of the Sermon on the Mount. There Jesus said,

> Blessed are those who are persecuted because of righteousness, for theirs is the kingdom of heaven. Blessed are you when people insult you, persecute you and falsely say all kinds of evil against you because of me. Rejoice and be glad, because great is your reward in heaven, for in the same way they persecuted the prophets who were before you (Matt. 5:10-12).

James's beatitude is different in a couple of areas from Matthew's. In the first place, nowhere in James is persecution the context of suffering. Although we cannot rule it out, if we include it, it would

be an argument from silence. In the second place, and more impor-
tantly, James's beatitude is pronounced not just on the person who is
tested and undergoes trials (or as in Matthew's case, who is persecuted) but upon the one who actively perseveres and endures. James's
intention, by this saying, is to encourage perseverance during this
period of intense suffering through which his community is going.

The blessing, which is assured the perseverer, has a tangible component. Those who have stood the test are promised a crown of life
(1:12). "What is this crown?" Is it a victor's crown—whether athletic or military prize? Or is it a royal crown, signifying the exalted
and eminent status of the receiver? Although a large number of Bible
students tend to see the context calling for the crown to be interpreted as a "prize" for the victor, we cannot rule out that the "royal"
meaning might have been in James's mind. Particularly, in light of
the fact that in the previous verses (vss. 9-11) he was dealing with
the theme of exaltation-humiliation. Yet, it might be best for us not
to speculate as to whether it is a victor's crown or a royal crown.
What we are sure of is that it is something that is promised to those
who love God (vs. 12).

The promise of a crown (or a "garland," as the word can be translated) as a reward goes back to Old Testament times. The book of
Proverbs has interesting examples in which the promise of a crown/
garland is joined with the bestowal of wisdom. For example, in the
opening exhortations to embrace wisdom, the wise man states that a
father's instructions and a mother's teaching "will be a garland to
grace your head and a chain to adorn your neck" (1:9). Later in the
book, wisdom is identified as a woman, who, if she is esteemed and
embraced, will "exalt you" and "honor you." But more than that,
"she will set a garland of grace on your head and present you with a
crown of splendor" (4:8, 9; see also 12:4; 16:31; 17:6).

James might have had this wisdom background in mind (his book
being so rich with the wisdom motif), but it is probably that he wishes
his readers to think about the crown in terms of the future eschatological rewards when the Lord comes. If this is true, then James
1:12 can be paralleled with The Wisdom of Solomon (an apocryphal book that was written approximately seventy-five years before

James's epistle) which says: "But the righteous live forever, and their reward is with the Lord; the Most High takes care of them. Therefore they will receive a glorious crown and a beautiful diadem from the hand of the Lord" (5:15, 16, NRSV). This eschatological focus is also found in biblical writings later than James. Paul is represented as saying at the end of his earthly existence, "I have fought the good fight, I have finished the race, I have kept the faith. Now there is in store for me the crown of righteousness, which the Lord, the righteous Judge, will award to me on that day—and not only to me, but also to all who have longed for his appearing" (2 Tim. 4:7, 8). It is in the letter to the church in Smyrna, however, that the juxtaposition of suffering and crown parallels James most evidently. The revelator quotes the Lord: "Do not be afraid of what you are about to suffer. I tell you, the devil will put some of you in prison to test you, and you will suffer persecution for ten days. Be faithful, even to the point of death, and I will give you the crown of life" (Rev. 2:10; see also 1 Pet. 5:4).

The interplay of suffering and crown has pervaded not only Christian thought throughout history but also artistic expressions within Christianity. Quite often we see the crown entwined with the cross—a symbolic expression that victory arises out of the endurance of trials. Many Christian martyrs throughout the centuries, as well as millions of Christians who underwent economic and social trials, were able to gain strength and sustenance from such promises as this one from Paul's writings: "I consider that our present sufferings are not worth comparing with the glory that will be revealed in us" (Rom. 8:18). So also today the child of God, while bearing the cross, looks forward to the crown. The symbolic cross may be physical—when a person's health is crippled; it may be economic—when there is no financial security or the imminent threat of loss of security; or it may be social and relational—when a spouse is unfaithful, abusive, or abandons the marriage. No matter what the symbolic cross or the trial, James calls for perseverance, and he promises a crown. The fact is, the true son and daughter of God will not stop loving God even when the tests and trials are most intense. That is why the crown is promised "to those who love Him" (1:12).

Blaming God

Earlier we noted that the word *peirasmos* can be translated "trials" as well as "temptation." Only the context can determine whether it refers to external afflictions or the inner enticement to sin. It seems that up to this point (1:13), James is primarily addressing external trials. Now he turns his attention specifically to internal temptations. We should note, however, that not all Bible scholars feel that we should accentuate the difference—at least some doubt that James intended to make such a distinction. For example, George Stulac suggests that "the temptations he [James] has in mind now are especially those that come in the context of his readers' trials—for example, the temptation to harbor hatred or to take revenge toward those who have persecuted them, or the temptation to be covetous and jealous in their economic hardship" (*James*, 53). Although Stulac may not be quite accurate in his identification of the trials in James, his point is well taken that the temptations could have arisen out of the trials.

Most likely what James is dealing with here is the sufferers' response to external trials. As his readers met their various trials, the challenge of James is, "How do you respond?" The trials they were facing possibly became occasions for temptation, and they in turn responded by attempting to pin the blame somewhere. This is quite understandable, because so often we blame our parents or some other person for what we have become. Or, we place the blame on circumstances for what we have done. Or, as Flip Wilson, the once-famous American comedian, popularized the phrase, "The devil made me do it!" It is true that people, circumstances, and even evil forces affect us, but persons in James's community seemed to have gone beyond that and were blaming God, saying: "God is tempting me" (vs. 13). They possibly thought that God was testing them with evil designs in mind or that God had given up on them and abandoned them to their fate. Or possibly they were simply struggling with their situation and could not understand God's role in it.

This raises the age-old question of theodicy—the attempts to reconcile the goodness and sovereignty of God with the existence of

evil—particularly as expressed by the question: Why do the righteous suffer? James's readers must have wondered aloud why do bad
experiences come about, just as we today struggle with the question
of how AIDS, cancer, cholera, earthquakes, hurricanes, warfare, etc.,
fit into the fact that God is good. Interestingly, James does not clear
up this issue of theodicy, although at this point it would be a most
opportune time to do so. Possibly, he does not consider it a serious
problem. Or, more likely, since the question is more theoretical
than practical, he is not interested in engaging it. He does not wish
to tackle the problem of whether a good God can permit evil; his
interest is in arguing that God is not the efficient cause of temptations. The root cause of temptation does not lie in God.

James is doing here what many Jewish writers had already done
in the past; namely, disassociate God from testing and temptation.
Let us note a couple of examples. In Genesis 22:1 we find the record
that God tested Abraham and told him to offer up his son Isaac.
However, in a pre-New Testament document (but post-Old Testament) it is Mastema, or Satan, not God, who tested Abraham (Jubilees 17:16). In the Jubilees' account, Satan is acting as a prosecutor,
as in the case of the Job narrative (see Job 1:6–2:8).

Even more significant is the differing accounts we find in 2 Samuel
and 1 Chronicles regarding who tempted, or incited, David to take a
census of his people. In 2 Samuel 24:1, the reporter clearly states that
"the anger of the Lord burned against Israel, and he incited David
against them, saying, 'Go and take a census of Israel and Judah.' "
However, in 1 Chronicles 21:1 it is not the Lord, but "Satan rose up
against Israel and incited David to take a census of Israel." This contradiction must be understood in light of the fact that in most ancient
cultures people attributed evil to demonic forces, the gods, or God.
In early Israel (when 2 Samuel was written) the Hebrew people did
not attribute events to demonic forces. For them, God was the author and originator of all things, both good and evil. When, on the
one hand, misfortune or calamities struck or negative orders were
given, or when, on the other hand, blessings were poured out or
positive commands were given, the source was always the almighty
Hebrew God, Yahweh. However, by the time 1 Chronicles was writ-

ten (some time after the Babylonian captivity), the Jewish people had developed a new perspective on who initiated good and who initiated evil. It was important to them at that time to protect God from any connection with evil. Therefore, it could not be God who incited or tempted David; it must have been Satan.

James, like these late authors and Jewish thinkers, disassociated God from testing and temptations. But unlike them, he does not put the blame on the devil either. He squarely lays moral accountability at the feet of the individual. This is possibly the strongest biblical affirmation of personal responsibility. This is precisely what James is saying when he writes, "Each one is tempted when, by his own evil desire, he is dragged away and enticed" (1:14).

In laying the blame on the individual, James most likely is relating to the rabbinic teaching of the "evil impulse," "evil inclination," or "evil instinct" (the *yetser hara*). It is this inner inclination that prods the person to sin. Some older Bible translations use the word *lust* in verse 14 to describe this inner impulse toward evil. However, we are mistaken if we understand James to be referring to temptations having sexual overtones. Today, the word *lust* has largely taken on a sexual connotation, but some centuries ago, it simply meant any strong desire or inclination. Modern English translations of the Bible usually use the word *desire* in verse 14. The concept in James and in Jewish rabbinic teaching goes beyond sexuality and is more closely related to an inner impulse resembling Freud's *id*. It is not the "self" or "ego." But it can control the "ego" and lead it into sin. (We should note here that in the New Testament the words *desire* and *lust* come from the same Greek word *epithumia*. Whether it is used positively, negatively, or neutrally is dependent on the context.

It is quite probable that Paul in Romans 7:7-23 is also close to the rabbinic teaching of the evil impulse that has mastered human beings since the Fall in the Garden of Eden. In these verses Paul speaks of the "I" or the "ego," which is doing just the opposite of what the spiritual nature desires. For example, he writes:

> I do not understand what I do. For what I want to do I do not do, but what I hate I do. . . . For I have the desire to do what is

good, but I cannot carry it out. For what I do is not the good I want to do; no, the evil I do not want to do—this I keep on doing (Rom. 7:15-19).

In Paul's argument, however, it is sin, not the "ego," that is the culprit: "Now if I do what I do not want to do, it is no longer I who do it, but it is sin living in me that does it (vs. 20). What Paul calls "sin" in this context is probably the same thing James calls "evil desire." Yet James's argument is not regarding sin and the inner struggle; it is about who takes the blame when there is temptation. For James, it is the individual's own evil desire.

In 1:14, 15 James employs a series of word pictures and metaphors to capture the essence of what happens when the evil impulse succeeds. First, in verse 14 he says that the person is dragged away and enticed. Simon Kistemaker suggests that here James is drawing from the art of fishing. "A fish sees the lure and is tempted to strike. When the fish takes hold of the bait, it is suddenly dragged away and pays with its life for its innocence and ignorance" (*James*, 49). But humans cannot claim ignorance and innocence. We are tempted by our own desires. James deprives us of any excuse to blame anything or anyone else. The cause lies within ourselves. The blame for the entrapment, the alluring, and the beguiling is personal.

In verse 15 James changes the word pictures and metaphors. Evil's progression now is graphically described in terms of the human reproductive process. (Of course, it is possible that verse 14 could be using the metaphor of a seducer or seductress enticing a person to bed, and that verse 15 pictures the outcome of that affair.) There is the process of "conception, incubation, gestation, and reproduction" (Martin, 32). But James does not stop at that. After birth there is maturity and death—disaster!

The picture James paints is dark. But his focus is not on the picture; it is on God. He wants to make it clear that God is not to be blamed for the enticements to do evil, which sometimes accompany trials. God does not initiate these trials and temptations. Rather, the blame must be placed within. James denies that powers outside ourselves—whether it be God, the devil, stars, or astrology—are the culprit. What he says parallels the famous line in Shakespeare's *Julius Caesar*: "The fault, dear Brutus, is not in our stars, but in ourselves." I can't any longer say that God, the stars, or even the devil made me do it! There will be no one to blame but myself.

Blessings From Above

James concludes this section (1:12-18) with a positive counterbalance to the negative assertions in verses 13-15. He has just made it clear that God is not the originator of temptations. Now he confirms this point with the positive. Temptations could not originate with God, because He sends only good from above (vs. 17). Furthermore, since He "does not change like shifting shadows" (vs. 17), it is impossible for Him to send evil. To believe otherwise—to deny that the blessings of "every good and perfect gift is from above, coming down from the Father of the heavenly lights" (vs. 17)—is to be totally deceived (vs. 16).

It is interesting that James includes the "heavenly lights" in this verse. Could it be, as Ralph Martin suggests, that his readers believed they were under the power of astral forces and fatalism, hence they doubted the goodness of God's character and regarded Him as no better than a finite being who was caught up in all the changes that were occurring? (31). If this suggestion has some credibility, then James is also counteracting such a belief and arguing the contrary. God is the creator of the luminaries and is uninfluenced by the countless changes that occur in the universe and the natural world. When one is tempted, James says don't blame God nor astrology nor fatalism nor any other powers. Rather, remember that only blessings come from God.

Let us not overlook too quickly two very important words James uses that highlight significant attributes of God—*perfect* and *change*. First, whatever statements we make about God must begin and end with the fact that He is perfect. Any definition of God that includes imperfection and evil is heresy. Therefore, it is impossible for God to be evil, do evil, or send evil. For James, then, this attribute of God excludes any element of evil in any and all gifts with which He blesses humanity. Second, this view of God's character remains consistent. Under no circumstance will God ever be imperfect. Therefore, He will always be the giver of good, and evil will never originate with Him.

James's argument ends with the most wonderful gift God has given—the creation of human beings. In verse 18 we find an antithetical parallelism with verse 15. In contrast to verse 15 where the evil impulse conceives, gives birth to sin, and produces death, verse 18 presents God in a feminine role as the One who gives us birth and who is the responsible agent in our being "a kind of firstfruits of all he has created." Thus the blessings from above are twofold—creation and new creation. Instead of blaming God, we must bless Him!

■ Applying the Word

James 1:12-18

1. Are there times when I have blamed God (or Satan) for trials or temptations, when, as I reflect back on the situation, I realize that neither should have been blamed? List two or three such instances.
2. Are there times when I deliberately or inadvertently used astrological signs to explain my behavior? Does the "sign" under which I was born have anything to do with my actions? Explain how this passage in James speaks to this issue.
3. In the past how have you answered the question, "Why do the righteous suffer?" Summarize how this study of James has helped you change or refine your understanding of the problem.
4. How do I deal with the "evil desire" within myself? Do I repent of its result and confess that the temptation comes from my own evil inclination? Or do I tend to ignore it or project it on something else? Explain.
5. Make a list of ten "good and perfect" gifts that God bestowed upon you this past week.

■ Researching the Word

1. Compare James 1:13 and Matthew 6:13. Do they contradict each other? Explain your answer. Look up Matthew 6:13 in a good Bible commentary. Is your explanation of the verse close to that of the commentary? If it is different, explain the difference(s).
2. In your concordance, look up the words *lust* and *desire* in the New Testament. (If you have a concordance with Greek lexical aids, e.g., Young's, Strong's, or *The NIV Exhaustive Concordance*, look up only those occurrences that are a translation of *epithumia*.) Select five passages for each word and analyze them. Which passages use the word positively? Which use the word negatively? Are there times when it is used neutrally? Do you disagree with any of the translations? List any such translations and explain why you disagree.
3. In question 1 of "Getting Into the Word" at the beginning of this chapter, you noted striking analogies to James 1:12-18 occurring elsewhere in the Bible—including, perhaps, many other texts that, like verse 17, state that God does not change. Now look at the texts given in the marginal references of Genesis 6:6. Do these passages teach a different theology from the ones cited in connection with James 1:17? Explain your conclusions.

■ Further Study of the Word

1. See *Thoughts From the Mount of Blessing*, 116-119, for E. G. White's comments on "temptations" and from whom they proceed.
2. For a detailed textual and historical study of the background of the "evil desire" in Judaism, see J. Marcus, "The Evil Inclination in the Epistle of James."
3. See R. P. Martin, *James*, for an overall, good commentary on these verses.

PART TWO

James 1:19–2:26

True
Religion

CHAPTER FOUR

Listening
and Doing

James 1:19-26

Part of James's epistle (1:1-18) introduces and focuses explicitly on the theme that underlines his concern throughout the document; namely, trials and suffering. Part 2 (1:19–2:26) continues his treatment of that theme. The emphasis here, however, is on defining true religion, particularly as it relates to those who are suffering. That is, how does the truly religious person relate to an individual who is undergoing trials, particularly economic trials?

At the heart of this section is the emphasis on doing. *A religion without action is useless. For James, religion is a "verb," not a "noun." Religion is not passive; it is active. An authentically religious person is one who moves beyond mere cognitive assent to some propositional truth or faith statement. The truly religious individual can be clearly identified by his or her practical actions.*

To introduce this most troublesome area of pastoral theology, James interjects the ethics of speech. Speech ethics was a most important theme in the Old Testament and later Jewish literature, and James will come back to it a number of times before he closes his letter. Here this ethic serves, in part, to demonstrate the inadequacies (and even the destructive nature) of speech vis-a-vis the importance and beneficial nature of "doing."

■ Getting Into the Word

James 1:19-26

Read verses 19-26 once. Then read it a second time within its immediate context—that is, read James, chapters 1 and 2. After you have done this, respond to the following exercises.

1. List in your James notebook two or three ways this passage (1:19-26) fits into the arguments of verses 1-18 and chapter 2.
2. Using a concordance, look up the word *angry* (and/or its cognates *anger*, *wrath*, etc.). Note the times it is used positively (for example, God's anger in the Old Testament) and instances when it is used negatively (for example, Jesus' saying in the Sermon on the Mount—Matt. 5:22). Explain why it is that anger seems good in some contexts and bad in others.
3. If you have access to different versions of the Bible, compare the various translations of 1:20. Did you find that some translated the latter part of the verse like the NIV—"The righteous life that God desires,"—while others translated the phrases "The righteousness of God" or "God's righteous purpose," etc.? How significant are these differing interpretive translations for James' immediate argument? Explain your answer.
4. In verse 21, James states that the "word" that is planted in a person can save that individual. Does this contradict Paul's teaching that states that a person is saved only by faith (Rom. 3:21-26)? Explain your answer.
5. Compare James's argument in 1:25 that the "law" gives freedom with Paul's position that the "law" holds persons in bondage and that it is faith that frees us (Gal. 3:23-25; Rom. 7). Explain the seeming contradiction.

■ Exploring the Word

Listening, Speaking, and Becoming Angry

Slow to speak, but quick to listen

James begins this section (1:19-26) with what could have been an original proverb: "Everyone should be quick to listen, slow to speak and slow to become angry" (vs. 19). Yet, like much of the proverbial sayings in this epistle, this one is similar to many found in the Old Testament and in popular Jewish oral traditions and teachings. For example, in Proverbs 13:3 the sage states: "He who guards his lips guards his life, but he who speaks rashly will come to ruin." We can note also the insightful saying of the Jewish religious leaders as found in Aboth 5:12 of the *Mishnah*: "There are four types of disciple: swift to hear and swift to lose—his gain is canceled by his loss; slow to hear and slow to lose—his loss is canceled by his gain; swift to hear and slow to lose—this is a happy lot; slow to hear and swift to lose— this is an evil lot." And in James's favorite apocryphal wisdom book the following is found: "If you love to listen you will gain knowl- edge, and if you pay attention you will become wise" (Sirach 6:33, NRSV). Even in Greek, non-Jewish literature we find parallels to James's saying. A classic one is cited by Martin Dibelius: In response to the question, "What is the best way to exercise authority," a high official is told: "Don't lose your temper! Do little talking and much listening!" (112).

James's intent is not to impose a vow of silence upon those of us who like to hear ourselves talking—who take delight in getting our point across in any conversation. The apostle simply wants us to be wise in the use of our mouths. Centuries before, the writer of Prov- erbs noted, "even a fool is thought wise if he keeps silent, and dis- cerning if he holds his tongue" (17:28). In many instances, listening is more important and has more advantages than speaking. The one who listens more and speaks less is the one who learns more and succumbs less to trouble. Lehman Strauss insightfully wrote: "God gave us two ears and only one mouth. Should we not be twice as swift to listen and learn? A wise man will listen to others and answer only if he is certain he has something worthwhile to say" (51). James wishes his audience to put listening, speaking, and anger in perspective. Eugene Petersen, in his paraphrased *The Message*, gives this proverb a contemporary slant and helps us to grasp James's perspective even more. He writes: "Post this at all the intersections, dear friends: Lead with your ears, follow up with your tongue, and let anger straggle along in the rear" (Prov. 1:19).

Slow to anger

It is interesting that James includes the issue of anger in his ethical admonitions regarding "speech" and "listening." Although at first sight this combination seems strange, yet in ancient wisdom literature the looseness of speech is often linked with anger that is not restrained. For example, Proverbs 17:27 states that "a man of knowledge uses words with restraint, and a man of understanding is even-tempered." The fact is, words spoken without careful thought often cause an outburst of anger and hot temper. In many instances, what begins as a friendly, intelligent discussion turns out to be an intense, uncontrollable, angry argument with the resulting flare of tempers. On the other hand, it is often the case that unrestrained, uncontrolled anger at someone leads a person to speak too quickly, say too much, and listen too slowly. James says: "Be quick to listen, slow to speak, and slow to become angry" (1:19).

Earlier we noted that the admonition "slow to speak" rules out a vow of silence, but it does indicate a call for wisdom in when and how to speak. The question for us is: Does the same hold true when James says we should be "slow to become angry"? If the phrases in the proverb are parallel, then James is not saying we should never become angry. James then would be admitting with modern psychologists that there is an anger that is healthy—an anger that is similar to the anger of God in the Old Testament and in Revelation (Carlson, 33-47).

On the other hand, we find that anger is not a positive emotion in the New Testament and in the contemporary Judaism of James's era. In the latter case, the rabbis taught that the angry person had not mastered his or her *yetser*. Furthermore, the rabbis held that one should not use God as an example in order to excuse one's own angry actions and emotions. The Jews believed there were certain divine qualities human beings were forbidden to imitate and that anger was one of these.

In the New Testament a couple of passages can be highlighted in which anger is unequivocally condemned. First, Jesus in the Sermon on the Mount equated anger with murder in the first of His six antitheses. He said, " 'You have heard that it was said to the people long ago, "Do not murder, and anyone who murders will be subject to judgment." But I tell you that anyone who is angry with his brother will be subject to judgment' " (Matt. 5:21, 22). And in the Colossian correspondence we find a clear injunction to "put to death . . . whatever belongs to your earthly nature" (Col. 3:5). Anger is listed among these sins, along with sexual immorality, idolatry, malice, filthy language, etc. (Col. 4:5-9).

The epistle to the Ephesians does seem, however, to have some ambivalence. It says, "In your anger do not sin: Do not let the sun go down while you are still angry, and do not give the devil a foothold" (Eph. 4:26, 27). Yet the apostle is quite precise when he writes a few verses later, "Get rid of all bitterness, rage and anger" (Eph. 4:31). I must admit that this duality, both here and in James, is difficult to comprehend in light of the New Testament's clear teaching against anger. I further don't believe that James is psychoanalyzing the emotion of anger. He is not addressing the healthful, emotional anger that modern psychologists encourage us to affirm. Possibly if James were writing to our twentieth- and twenty-first century western societies, he might agree with the psychological theorists. However, as I read rigorously these New Testament texts, it seems to me that the anger they are dealing with is heavily impregnated with sin and should be avoided.

Some interpret James's admonition "slow to become angry" to be a statement that does allow *some* anger; namely, righteous indignation. That may be so. The fact is, however, that too often we excuse our profane temper by calling it righteous indignation. This so-called righteous indignation in many instances is simply self-centered irritation and ego-centered anger. Behavioral scientists tell us that some angry behavior (which some of us Christians excuse as righteous indignation) is simply a result of frustration. And some of the frustration is a result of not getting our own way. It has nothing to do with the righteousness of God, truth, or justice.

In view of James's overall theme, this proverb should be read in the light of his concern for the trials and suffering of his community. Many people get angry at others because of the stress and trials of everyday life. Thus the pressures of trials in James's community might have made his readers or hearers slow to listen and quick to speak, especially quick to speak in anger. This is quite easy for us to understand, as Stulac notes in his illustration of contemporary life: "A married couple struggling financially is more likely to experience marital conflict. They may fight over the money or over other issues, but the financial trial has become the occasion for sinning against each other" (*James*, 64). In the case of James, anger may have been destroying the peace of his community. It may even have been part of the "quarrels and fights" of James 4:1, 2. Whatever it may be, anger can destroy communal harmony.

It is interesting to note that in this section James speaks about accepting "the word" (1:21) and listening "to the word" (vs. 22). This has led many to see "the word" as that which James's readers have been talking about and fighting about. Admittedly, when James urges his readers to "be quick to listen, slow to speak and slow to become angry" (vs. 19), he doesn't specifically say that it is "the word" that they should be slow to speak about and quick to listen to. Furthermore, the prohibition against quick anger does not fit snugly with the idea that it is "the word" that is at the heart of the anger in the community. But the idea can be easily extrapolated into our modern Christian experience. In too many of our churches, members find in the Word (the Scriptures) little else than subjects for debate. The debates, disputes, quarrels, and angry confrontations among members, which destroy communal harmony, frequently center around our theology and biblical interpretations, while the mission of the church suffers. My colleague, Alden Thompson, is certainly correct when he notes that "theology divides; mission unites." James would admonish us today to be "slow to speak," "quick to listen," and "slow to become angry," even in the arena of theological and biblical interpretive discussions.

In the next verse following these maxims (vs. 20), James makes it clear that the anger he is writing about is certainly not the positive anger we moderns hold up as emotionally healthful. This verse seems to support the contention that the phrase "slow to become angry" should be interpreted differently from the earlier phrase "slow to speak." "To speak" is not something negative. James is simply saying one's speech should be careful and restrained and that on the spectrum between "listening" and "speaking," one should listen more. But anger is different. If verse 20 is used to interpret verse 19, we must admit that the anger James is speaking of is totally negative. Such an active emotion as he perceives anger to be should never be practiced. James states categorically, "A man's anger does not bring about the righteous life that God desires" (vs. 20).

A note on righteousness

We must pause to ask the question, What does James mean when he uses the term "righteous" in the phrase "the righteous life that God desires" (NIV)? We should note that the NIV translation of this phrase is an interpretation; the Greek reads simply, "God's righteousness." A literal translation of verse 20 is: "For the anger of man does not work (or bring about) the righteousness of God." The phrase, "the righteousness of God," is not clear as it stands and thus needs some interpretation even in its translation, as the NIV rightly attempts to do.

There are a number of ways of understanding "righteousness." But before we highlight those, it should be noted that the Greek word *dikaiosynē* and the Hebrew *tsedeq*, along with their cognates (which we usually translate "righteousness"), can also be translated right(eous)ness, or just(ice). With this in mind, the first possible interpretation of the phrase is "the righteous status that God bestows upon us." This translation attempts to impose an understanding of righteousness as a status that is conferred upon the Christian—an understanding that many modern interpreters find narrow and faulty. (See the commentary by John Brunt on Romans in the Bible Amplifier series.) However, as I will continue to emphasize in this volume, we should be extremely careful in attempting to interpret James through the eyes of Paul.

A second way to understand the phrase is in the sense given by the NIV, that is, the righteous activity or the righteous life that meets with God's approval. Although this understanding is not explicit in the phrase, the context does allow it. In the first place, the entire epistle attempts to lay out ethical admonitions for righteous living. In the second place, the immediate context of verses 19 and 21 deals specifically with the righteous (or in contrast, the unrighteous) life.

In the third place, Peter Davids notes that this passage may be tied in with James 3:8-12, where there is a condemnation for cursing one's brother. Davids notes that since 1:19 deals with speech and so do the verses in chapter 3, it is possible that the angry outbursts (1:19) and the cursing of men (3:9) are references to the same unrighteous acts. The sense then would be that these angry outbursts of cursing would not reflect the standard of righteousness that God demands (see Davids, *Commentary*, 93; compare Davids, *James*, 40).

"Justice," however, is also a valid interpretation of the Greek word *dikaiosynē* which may have some merit here. Within this understanding there are two possibilities; the first is what can be called eschatological, or God's future justice. It is possible that James has in mind here the eschatological justice of God that is brought to view in 5:7. There he encourages his readers and hearers to wait patiently upon God, who will bring about the final judgment and who will act decisively and justly.

Second, James may not have in mind here the "justice of God," but rather, the life of justice that God desires of human beings. E. Malcolm Sidebottom has rightly noted that in Jewish thought "righteousness" is not seen only in the sense of strict piety and uprightness as we think about those concepts today. He says "it embraces also the 'goodness' that we know of in God in the sense of beneficence and benevolence." He then goes on to suggest that "coming so closely after the enunciation of the doctrine of God's invariable goodness, the word must have this meaning here" (33). If this is the meaning here, and if this is what God desires of humans, then

James is saying exactly what Micah, the Old Testament prophet of social justice, said in the eighth century B.C.: "He has showed you, O man, what is good. And *what does the Lord require of you? To act justly* and to love mercy and to walk humbly with your God" (Mic. 6:8). To act justly is to act with beneficence and benevolence. This will become even more clear when we read James's strong social-justice stance (one very similar to Micah's) a few verses below (1:27; chapter 2 in its entirety; and 5:1-6). James may already be arguing here that a person's anger can prevent him or her from acting justly as God acts justly.

The nature of "moral filth" and being saved

After focusing on listening, speech, and anger, James concludes this paragraph with a call to get rid of, or put away, moral filth and evil. This admonition is widely used in the New Testament. In the ethical imperative section of the Epistle to the Romans (chapters 12–15), Paul places this admonition in an eschatological context: "The night is nearly over; the delay is almost here. So let us put aside the deeds of darkness" (13:12). Ephesians, on the other hand, places this ethical imperative in the context of the believer's initial coming to Christ: "You were taught, with regard to your former way of life, to put off your old self" (4:22; compare vs. 25); while Colossians gives the admonition under the rubric of holy living in Christ: "But now you must rid yourselves of all such things as these: anger, rage, malice, slander, and filthy language from your lips" (3:8). Other passages of note that emphasize the same concern include Hebrews 12:1 ("Therefore, since we are surrounded by such a great cloud of witnesses, let us throw off everything that hinders") and 1 Peter 2:1 ("Therefore, rid yourselves of all malice and all deceit, hypocrisy, envy, and slander of every kind"). James, without listing specific sins as do most of the other New Testament epistles, simply states "get rid of all moral filth and the evil that is so prevalent" (1:21).

James 1:21 is the only place in the New Testament where the word that is here translated "filth" is used as a noun—although in 2:2 it is used as an adjective with reference to a person wearing filthy rags. In the Greek translation of the Old Testament (LXX or

Septuagint), the word is used in the discussion of Joshua the High Priest, whose filthy garments were taken away and who was clothed with new ones (Zech. 3:4). Because of this similarity, it is possible that by calling for the renunciation of moral filth James is also using the metaphor of a soiled or dirty garment. Ralph P. Martin, however, has suggested that the word could be construed in a specialized sense as a medical term for earwax, which needs to be washed away to give good hearing. This would nicely fit the context of listening and speaking (48).

Whether the metaphor involves filthy clothes or undesirable earwax, James's point is clear: such a lifestyle must be gotten rid of. And James goes on to add that his readers would do well to put off "the evil that is so prevalent" (1:21). Although the word *evil* (*kakias*) could be understood in its basic meaning of "evil" and "bad," it has been suggested that it could be better translated here as "malice." Thus the phrase would be translated "every trace of malice" or "malice which is so abundant" (see Davids, *James*, 40). James would thus be attacking not only external anger but also the inner malice that of necessity must be dispelled from the heart and soul.

Does the command to "get rid of" or "put off" mean that we can accomplish this with our own strength and willpower? Do *we* get rid of the filth, the evil, the malice, or is it *Christ* who does it for us? James's imperative needs to be understood in light of the general teaching of Scripture, which indicates that we cannot do good in our own strength. Any attempt to live the godly life by lifting ourselves by our own bootstraps or to vindicate ourselves before God by our own ability to put away sin is doomed to fail. The text in Isaiah 64:6 is clear: "All our righteous acts are like filthy rags." One cannot put away "filthy rags" by using a filthy-rag method. The narrative in Zechariah 3 of Joshua the High Priest makes it clear that it was not Joshua who took off his filthy clothes; they were taken off for him. Thus the angel of the Lord could say, " 'See, I have taken away your sin, and I will put rich garments on you' " (Zech. 3:4).

James first states the negative: Get rid of filth and evil. Next he states the positive: "Humbly accept the word planted in you, which can save you" (1:21). Before we can deal with the issue as to whether or not "the word" saves, let us identify the "word" (*logos* in the Greek). In John 1:1, Jesus is identified as the Word, the Logos. But it is doubtful that James has the Johannine perspective in mind. He is hardly speaking here about the indwelling Christ, even though this would make excellent theology. The picture of Jesus as the Logos is limited to John's prologue (John 1:1-18) in the New Testament, and the concept of the indwelling Christ is more of a Pauline idea. Probably, James is using "the word" as synonymous with "the law," that is, the Old Testament Scriptures.

The larger question looming before us is this: Do the implanted Scriptures really save or bring salvation? Is a person saved or justified on the grounds of confessing the Word? Aren't we saved by grace through faith and not by works or words of any kind? It may be difficult to answer these questions in light of James's statement if we understand the word "to save" (*sōzō*) in the same manner in which Paul uses it in his theological discussions of righteousness by faith. But the verb "to save" does not merely imply personal soul salvation. In many instances, particularly in the Gospels, it has reference to restoration of life and physical healing. For example, after the woman who had the flow of blood for twelve years touched Jesus' garment, Jesus said to her, "Daughter, your faith has healed [*sōzō*] you" (Luke 8:48). If this is the sense in which James is using the word "to save," then he is saying that what the word does is to make one whole and complete in totality.

James states that his readers are to *humbly* accept this "word" (1:21). This humility and meekness is the antithesis to the anger he earlier spoke about. In contrast to the anger that does not bring about the righteous, or just, life that God desires, James pleads for humility as his readers accept the word. We can conclude this section by noting that in James's three-part proverb (vs. 19), he is leading his readers from best to not-too-bad to worst ethical action: Listening is best—be quick to do it; speaking is not too bad—be slow to do it; anger is bad—be slow to become angry because it is really ungodly and is the opposite of the humility with which we should accept the word that makes one whole.

Listening Versus Doing

James does not wish his readers to succumb to the self-deception that mere listening to the Word is the highest ethical action. He commands: "Do not merely listen to the word, and so deceive yourselves. Do what it says" (vs. 22). With this, James comes to the heart of his argument within this section (vss. 19-26): At the root of true religion there is action—doing. To make his point, James uses the "listening-doing" (or "hearing-doing") antithesis, which was common in popular ethical discourse. In an oral culture such as that of James, most learning and communication was done orally, so it was natural for "listen" to be the first half of the antithesis. Had James been writing today, he might not only admonish against simply hearing or listening but against mere reading or watching as well, since our culture is a visual one. The emphasis in this paragraph is not on listening and the usage of other such senses, but on *doing*. That is James's principal admonition, the centerpiece of his concern. His readers cannot be content with a mere passive listening to the Word. True religion is essentially a life that is active, one that builds on what is heard.

James's focus echoes the conclusion of Jesus in the Sermon on the Mount when He said "Everyone who hears these words of mine and puts them into practice is like a wise man who built his house on the rock. . . . But everyone who hears these words of mine and does not put them into practice is like a foolish man who built his house on sand" (Matt. 7:24-26). Thus for both Jesus and James, hearing or listening is important, but more important is doing what is taught by Jesus, or doing what "the word" says. This is the critical point James wishes to highlight.

James makes this point both in the negative and in the positive. First, in the negative, by outlining the nature of the person who does not do what the word says. And second, in the positive, by stating the blessing the doer of the word will gain (1:23-25).

James uses the illustration of a mirror to present his case. The figure of the mirror is also found in 1 Corinthians 13:12, where there is a contrast between the imperfect knowledge gained through reflection and the perfect knowledge of reality in the future ("Now we see but a poor reflection as in a mirror, then we shall see face to face. Now I know in part; then shall I know fully, even as I am fully known"). James's concern is not about knowledge gained—whether imperfect or perfect, but on what is done with that knowledge.

The illustration in James 1:23, 24 is that of a man (the Greek uses the word for "male" rather than the generic word for a person; possibly there is something manly about the illustration!) who looks at his face in a mirror but soon forgets what he looks like after he moves away from the mirror. It is of interest to note that ancient mirrors were not made of glass but of highly polished metal. These metal objects rested flat on a table, so that in order to look at one's face a person had to bend over and peer down into the mirror.

Because in verse 25 James draws the contrast by speaking about a person who "looks intently" into the perfect law, it has been suggested that the man in verses 23, 24 merely gives a sideways glance or that he is like one who is peeping out of a window and does not wish to be seen (Mayor, 69, 70). The contrast, then, is between a hasty glance and a sustained gaze. But others argue that the intent of the gaze, or the lack thereof, is not James's interest. His concern is what happens after the looking experience.

It is a reality of life that a person's face is never the same from day to day. It changes as it reflects the experiences of life. A person is certainly foolish if he or she goes to the mirror to observe his or her looks but refuses to respond to the facial changes the mirror indicates. How can a person operate during the day on the basis of an image of himself or herself that is at odds with the physical reality the mirror portrayed? Such a person is unnatural. So also is the unnaturalness of hearing the Word, which does not result in appropriate action.

Verse 25 presents the wise and opposite person. This one takes the time and trouble to look intently into what is heard or seen. This one considers its implications for practical living and action.

This person is benefited because he or she acts in accordance with what is seen in the mirror.

For James, the mirror is what he calls the "perfect law that gives freedom." We noted earlier that "law" in this verse is possibly a synonym for "the word" used in verses 21-23. Although in many instances in the New Testament "law" (*nomos*) is equivalent to the Torah (the first five books of the Old Testament), it seems that James has in mind the entire Scriptures as he knew it then, or the entire corpus of God's will—His Word. It is this Word, this law, that is perfect. James's thought has close similarities with that of the psalmist, who wrote: "The law of the LORD is perfect" (Ps. 19:7).

James states that this law gives freedom (1:25). This might seem to contradict Paul, who states that the law holds a person in bondage (see Gal. 3:23-25). However, we must always keep in mind that Paul and James are discussing law in two entirely different contexts. For the most part, when Paul is speaking against "law," his reference is to "works of law" (see the discussion beginning on page 113 on 2:14-26). On the other hand, James argues, as do many Jewish teachers, that the law is not a constraint but gives us true freedom to do God's will—a freedom from ourselves and our self-interest, a release to love our neighbors and to serve them. This interpretation of James's understanding of the content of the law will be made unequivocally clear in 1:27–2:26. But for now he simply gives a benediction on those who do what the Word says: They will be blessed in what they do (1:25).

Speaking and Worthless Religion

James is anxious to get into a detailed discussion of what he means when he admonishes his readers to do what the Word says. This he will get to in verse 27 and in chapter 2. In 1:27 he summarizes what true religion is, with special emphasis on taking care of those persons on the margins of society. Chapter 2 gives a detailed commentary on what that means.

However, before James gives an example of true religion, he briefly suggests an example of worthless religion. This he does in 1:26. This verse serves also as a link between verses 19-25 and 1:27–2:26. It is possible to see "self-deception" as the actual term linking these passages; that is, self-deception is applicable to the person in 1:24 and the individual in verse 26. Or it is possible to argue that verse 26 serves as the connecting link by demonstrating a specific example in which obedience to the Word is not manifested. James seems to be reverting to his three-part proverb (vs. 19) and dealing with the one part he has so far said nothing about. He has dealt with anger at length and has followed that with a discussion on the inadequacies of listening. Now he must address speaking briefly (and he will return to it at length in chapter 3). This he will do in the context of true versus worthless religion.

For James, a person who is self-deceived considers himself or herself religious but who is not "slow to speak" (vs. 19); that is, one who does not keep a tight rein on the tongue. His or her religion is worthless (vs. 26). As will be seen in chapter 3 of his epistle, James regards the control of the tongue of utmost importance.

It seems strange that James considers tongue-control as evidence of being truly religious. The words used here for "religion" and "religious" usually describe scrupulous attention to details of formal worship, prayer, fasting, systematic giving—in short, religious duties, observances, ceremonies, and exercises. But James critiques such a limited definition of religion by arguing for a different type of religion.

James's critique is similar to that of the prophets (Isa. 1:10-17; Jer. 7:21-28; Hos. 6:6), and particularly Jesus, who was very critical of the mere outward observances of prescribed forms of religion—whether it be giving alms to the needy, praying, or fasting as the Pharisees did (Matt. 6:1-8).

True religion goes beyond these forms. All these religious activities are considered worthless in James's book if the so-called religious individual cannot keep a tight rein on his or her tongue. True religion involves self-control. If his readers can master their speech, they have taken an enormous step toward self-control. It is only then that their religion is worthwhile. With this stated clearly, James can now move on to what it means to *do* true religion.

■ Applying the Word

James 1:19-26

1. Make a list of things, not found in this passage, in which it is good or advantageous to be "quick" and another list of things in which it is well to be "slow." List also specific incidents in your experience when these items were pertinent to your situation.
2. Does the admonition "slow to speak" apply to oral witnessing for Christ? Have you found in your experience times when it was not appropriate to *talk* about Jesus? If Yes, list examples of such occasions and explain why. If No, do you think such an occasion could arise? Explain your answer.
3. Are there times when I should openly and clearly express my angry feelings? If Yes, what are some examples of such times? If No, how do I respond to those who say "anger" is a God-given emotion that must be expressed appropriately?
4. When I look in the mirror of my life each day, do I find things I want to change? What are some of those things?
5. Do I find myself quite scrupulous in my religious and church duties—both in action and language, yet quite careless in my day-to-day activities and speech? As I reflect on this past week, do I find my "Sabbath personality" to be quite different from my "Sunday-to-Friday personality"? If Yes (in even the least particular), list ways in which improvement can be made.

■ Researching the Word

1. Use your concordance and/or simply browse through Proverbs and find as many texts as possible that address the issues of "slow to speak" and "quick to listen." List them in your notebook. Make notes on any similarities, additional teachings, or differences with James's teaching in 1:19.
2. Using a concordance, look up the word *save* or its cognates

(salvation, saviour). Make a list of different and distinct uses of the term. Next, look up the word(s) in a Bible dictionary. List other usages of the word(s) you missed in your earlier search.

■ Further Study of the Word

1. For an excellent study on how to deal with anger, see D. Augsburger, *Caring Enough to Confront: How to Understand and Express Your Deepest Feelings Toward Others.*
2. Another book of the same nature as the one above is D. L. Carlson, *Overcoming Hurts and Anger: How to Identify and Cope With Negative Emotions.*
3. For some of E. G. White's views on anger and reconciliation, see *Thoughts From the Mount of Blessing,* 55-59.

CHAPTER FIVE

Caring for the Poor

James 1:27–2:26

The second chapter of James's epistle contains a number of verses and significant arguments that have made the document both famous and infamous. It is verses within this chapter that caused Martin Luther, the sixteenth-century Protestant reformer, to disparage the value of the book and its theology. For Luther and for millions who followed him through the centuries, 2:14-26 was, and still is, a stumbling block to the true freedom of the gospel—a freedom that is clearly explicated in Paul's writing, a freedom that involves faith alone without any works at all. Thus, for James to say that one is justified by works and not by faith alone is suspect theology, bordering on heresy.

The issue of faith and works is not the only controversial aspect of this chapter. In the history of Christendom the first part of the chapter has possibly had a longer controversial life. The subtle, and not so subtle, attacks James makes on the rich and his overt, unquestionable support for the poor has made his epistle unpopular among Christians who find themselves in the camp of the wealthy. Today, those who hold a high view of Scripture are not prepared to throw this passage out or relegate it to the back of the Bible; instead, this solid teaching of James is either ignored or spiritualized to the point of losing its force and bite. We need to recapture James's teaching with all its intensity, even if it offends our modern sensibilities.

We need to hear also the entire argument of James in chapter 2. Sadly, we have separated the first half of the chapter from the second. We read and interpret both as if they were two completely independent arguments. But James is not making a socioeconomic argument in the first half and a theological argument devoid of socioeconomic concerns in the second. On the contrary, his entire argument is a seamless one that focuses on his readers' concern and care for the poor. This discussion, in reality, does not commence in chapter 2 but is introduced in 1:27. James's position is that true religion, one that holds faith and works in tandem, looks after the poor and marginal in their distress and sufferings.

■ Getting Into the Word

James 1:27–2:13

Read through 1:27–2:26 once, then 1:27–2:13 twice. Now complete the following exercises:

1. Make two columns in your notebook. In the first column, list as many things and actions as you can think of that characterize true religion (including those mentioned in James 1:27). In the second column, list some characteristics of false religion.

2. Many religious denominations require those who join the church to make a commitment to "keep themselves from being polluted by the world" (vs. 27) as part of their doctrinal statement. After reading these verses, do you think that one of the fundamental beliefs and practices of the church should be taking care of the social needs of those in distress? Explain.

3. Before reading this passage, did you view meeting the social and economic needs of the marginal to be central and obligatory to your personal faith and/or the faith of the church? Or did you see it as peripheral and optional? If your mind has changed, to what degree has it changed?

4. Compare 2:2, 3 with Jesus' teaching in the Sermon on the Mount regarding treasure and clothing (Matt. 6:19-34). How do these texts in James and Matthew relate to each other?

5. Does 2:5 really say that God has a preferential option for the poor? Explain your understanding of what the verse is saying.

6. What particular commandment do you think James is referring to in verse 10 when he says that if a person stumbles in one, he is guilty of breaking the entire law?
7. Explain why James chose the commandments of adultery and murder to illustrate his arguments (vs. 11)?
8. List at least five explicit or implicit reasons James gives why his readers should not show favoritism to the rich at the expense of the poor.

■ Exploring the Word

True Religion

In a sense, the last verse of chapter 1 governs the thought of the unit that precedes it as well as of the passage that follows it. In the preceding verses, particularly 1:22-25, James's focus is on *doing*. Here in verse 27 he makes a statement regarding the doer that acts. This statement is illustrated by the entire argument of chapter 2. In all these verses, James is concerned with the nature of the truly religious person in relation to his or her concern for the poor and marginal.

As in 1:26, James gives what we might consider to be an unconventional definition of true and pure religion. The word translated "religion" (*thrēskeia*) can also be translated "worship." For the most part, when we think of these two words, our thoughts conjure up images of a certain type of person performing certain types of acts in a church setting. William Barclay, however, says it well when he writes that real worship, as far as God is concerned, does not "lie in elaborate vestments or in magnificent music or in a carefully wrought service; it lies in the practical service of mankind and in the purity of one's own personal life. It is perfectly possible for a Church to be so taken up with the beauty of its buildings and the splendour of its liturgy, that it has neither the time nor the money for practical Christian service" (61). This is not to say it is wrong to have the noblest and most splendid worship in a special place dedicated to such an enterprise. But as Barclay says further, "all such worship is empty and idle unless it sends a man out to love God by loving his fellow-man" (62).

The teaching that outward religiosity and the rituals of formal worship are vain if they are devoid of care and concern for people in need is not new. James is simply repeating what both Jesus and the prophets emphasized. Prophets such as Isaiah, Micah, Amos, Hosea, and Zechariah were particularly obsessed with this issue—especially were they open to the defense of widows and orphans. Isaiah begins his book with an attack on the leaders of Jerusalem, referring to them as "rulers of Sodom" and "people of Gomorrah" (1:10). He makes it quite clear that God has no pleasure in their sacrifices and offerings (vss. 11, 12), their special holy days (vss. 13, 14), nor even their prayers on such occasions (vs. 15). Instead, he implores them to "wash and make yourselves clean. Take your evil deeds out of my sight! Stop doing wrong, learn to do right! Seek justice, encourage the oppressed. *Defend the cause of the fatherless, plead the cause of the widow*" (vss. 16, 17). Later in the book, he further argues that true fasting is loosening the chains of injustice, letting the oppressed go free, sharing food with the hungry, providing shelter for the homeless, and clothing the naked (58:6, 7).

Isaiah's eighth-century contemporary in Jerusalem echoes the same concerns. For Micah, God really is not interested in burnt offerings and other ritualistic gifts. What He requires is "to act justly, to love mercy, and to walk humbly with your God" (6:6-8). Amos uses even stronger language. He quotes God as saying, "I hate, I despise your religious feasts; I cannot stand your assemblies. . . . Away with the noise of your songs! I will not listen to the music of your harps. But let justice roll on like a river, righteousness like a never-failing stream!" (5:21-24; Hos. 6:6). Even after the Babylonian captivity we find prophets such as Zechariah singing the same refrain: "This is what the Lord Almighty says: 'Administer true justice; show mercy and compassion to one another. Do not oppress the widow or the fatherless, the alien or the poor' " (7:9, 10).

The prophets were not the only defenders of the poor, widows, and orphans. We find even the psalmist proclaiming "A father to the fatherless, a defender of widows, is God in his holy dwelling"

(Ps. 68:5; compare Deut. 10:18). The story of Jesus in the Gospels also demonstrates the Messiah's constant defense of such marginal people. Some of His strongest statements are found in Mark, where He agrees with the teacher of the law who stated that to love one's neighbor "is more important than all burnt offerings and sacrifices" (12:33). And later in the same chapter we find one of His strongest condemnations of the Pharisees, when he accused them of embezzling from the widows and thus enriching themselves (vs. 40).

James, like the prophets, the psalmist, and Jesus is also sensitive to the poor widows and orphans. These, possibly, are not the only groups of poor that James is interested in. They are mentioned and highlighted, I believe, because they were proverbial in the ancient world as symbols of those who were exploited, defenseless, and poor. They had no one to protect them from the preying, unscrupulous person. They were the helpless in society. They were like those people today "who suffer from want in the third world, in the inner city; those who are unemployed and penniless; those who are inadequately represented in government or in law" (Moo, 86). To help these in their distress is James's definition of pure and faultless religion.

Chapter 1 ends with what seems to be a further definition of pure and faultless religion: "to keep oneself from being polluted by the world" (vs. 27). This is normally interpreted to mean that along with service to the poor James's readers should strive for personal holiness (Tasker, 55) and may have led some to asceticism and reclusiveness from the "world" or society. James, however, most likely is not arguing for some individualistic, overly personal religion. The "world," for James, is not the society apart from the community he is writing to. Bruce Johanson has noted that, in James, "world" may be taken to mean a "widespread disposition and power in mankind for evil in opposition to God" (119). The term *world*, then, is the whole scheme of things, values, and actions that separate us from God and that is at odds with what God requires. It is not limited to the social, but neither does it exclude a social sense. And although James may have a personal sense in mind, it is more likely in this context that the overriding sense is social.

To keep oneself from being polluted by the world is to avoid being tainted by the prevailing value system that is in opposition to God's desires. In the context of James, such a value system depreciates the poor and marginal. By worldly standards, sensitivity to the poor was not a priority. If James's community follows *this* value system, they will find themselves in alliance with those who live a life incompatible with God. Again, we must emphasize that we are not denying the inward-looking, individualistic, personal aspect of true religion. The problem comes when we focus on the personal aspect at the expense of social, horizontal religion. If we ignore this latter aspect of the religious life, our religion is faulty, impure, and polluted.

Faulty Religion Illustrated

Chapter 2 clearly illustrates, in the negative, what James considers pure and faultless religion to be. Here he indicts his audience's preference for the rich and in so doing continues his crusade on behalf of the poor. As we have noted earlier, in just about all the passages in which the issue of rich and poor is treated, the subject of James's censure is the rich. However, in this passage it is those who lack sensitivity to the poor who are condemned. This condemnation is even more intensified because, on the part of some, there is a display of prejudice in favor of the rich.

James begins the passage by addressing his readers personally: "My brothers, as believers in our glorious Lord Jesus Christ" (vs. 1). We must note that the phrase translated in the NIV, "believers in our glorious Lord Jesus Christ," literally reads "the faith of [or in] our Lord Jesus Christ." The NIV interprets the Greek phrase to mean *persons* who have faith in Jesus. But there is strong evidence that it should be translated to refer to those who possess a *faith* like Jesus. The faith of Jesus was one of obedience to His Father. Beside the fact that this Greek phrase is best translated as *faith of* in the New Testament—even in Paul's writing (see Maynard-Reid, *Poverty and Wealth*, 50, 51; 117, 118)—it is noteworthy that this translation of the text in James makes much more contextual sense when it is paralleled with the preceding verses in 1:22-27. In those verses, the call is to active obedience. Here in this illustration, James is saying that if his audience had such a faith, they would stop showing favoritism.

James's readers were in the habit of being partial. Interestingly, showing partiality to the rich was not the only type of favoritism they practiced. The fact is that the Greek word for favoritism is in the plural. This indicates that there were various partialities being manifested in the community. James appeals to his readers to stop such unfairness. Literally, he is prohibiting the continuation of actions or conditions that are in progress or existing. James begs them to stop practicing this negative behavior.

This perversion of true religion can be equated to our modern concept of discrimination. Persons in James's community were practicing social snobbery that went counter to the character of God that Jesus displayed in His life. In this illustration, James provides us with an example of how seriously he and the early church leaders addressed problems of this nature. The text gives us a paradigm as to how we can, and possibly should, deal with snobbery and discrimination today (Smit, 66).

The illustration we have in front of us is that of two persons coming into a "meeting" place and each being treated differently (2:2-4). If we are to grasp the social impact of this narrative, it is necessary to have it in its correct setting. The word translated "meeting" literally is "synagogue" in the Greek. If we are not tied to the view that James is writing specifically to a local Christian church but rather to Jews in general who, as Jesus did, professed faith in God and His word, then we need not read this text as having reference to a Christian meeting. Rather, its reference is to the synagogue building that both Christians and non-Christian Jews attended in the very early days of Palestinian Christianity.

If James is referring to the actual synagogue meeting place, we must next identify the purpose of the gathering. Synagogues were used not only for religious rites and meetings but for transaction of business for political gatherings. But they were also used for judicial proceedings. Jesus' statement in Luke 12:11 "When you are brought before synagogues, rulers, and authorities, do not worry about how you will defend yourselves or what you will say . . ." suggests a legal proceeding.

Apart from Jesus' statement and other New Testament evidence, there are many references in Jewish writings that suggest that synagogues were used as courts of law. Let us illustrate with two rabbinic texts that clearly give a judicial background for James's illustration. The first speaks about two persons attending court, one dressed in rags and the other richly attired. The Jewish text states: "How do we know that, if two come to court, one clothed in rags and the other in fine raiment worth a hundred *manehs*, they ['the court'] should say to him [the well-dressed man] 'Either dress like him, or dress him like you?' " (Maynard-Reid, "Poor and Rich, 169).

The second rabbinic text deals with the issue of sitting and standing in court. In Jewish courts, judges sit, and litigants stand. "Rabbah, son of R[abbi] Huna said: If a rabbinical scholar and an illiterate person have some dispute with each other, and come to court, we persuade the rabbinical scholar to sit; and to the illiterate person we also say, 'sit,' and if he stands, it matters not. Rab, son of R[abbi] Sherabya, had a case before R[abbi] Papa. He told him to sit, and told his opponent also to sit; but the court [attendant] came and nudged [literally, 'kicked'] the illiterate man and made him stand up" (Maynard-Reid, "Poor and Rich," 170).

The parallels between these two rabbinic texts and James 2:2, 3 are striking. The poor, shabbily clothed person in verse 2 is similar to the person clothed in rags in the rabbinic text. And the person with gold rings and fine clothes in verse 3 parallels the individual in fine raiment. So also in the second rabbinic example, the practice of giving a seat to the "superior one" is forbidden; yet the very thing is done by the court attendant, as well as by those in James's community, who give a seat to the wealthy and tell the poor person to stand.

When we come to the realization that James's illustration is placed in a nonreligious setting, we will view the issue of discrimination in a different perspective. There are those who argue that in the worship setting we are all equal—"at the foot of the cross we stand equal!"—but that in society we are not. Thus we can treat people civilly in church but have racist or class-denigrating attitudes toward them outside of church in everyday life. James's position is that favoritism, prejudice, partiality, and discrimination have no place in the church or society, in the worship setting or during judicial proceedings.

James's concern was specifically about the deference shown to the rich. Although the words *rich* or *wealthy* are not used in the passage, it seems evident that he is referring to such persons in verses 2, 3. The practice of wearing rings and expensive clothing was popular not only throughout the non-Jewish Roman Empire but also in Palestine. In the parable of the Prodigal Son (which I prefer to call "The Patient Father"—Luke 15:11-32), the wayward, returning son is given the best robe and a ring. Throughout the Roman Empire there was a wanton display of wealth—clothes bedecked with expensive gems and ornaments. In Jerusalem we find the extravagance of the rich—their houses, clothes, rich offerings—in contrast with the marginal poor. These wealthy had the cards stacked in their favor. And as James seems to indicate, the poor had come to court to seek justice. But the chances of gaining a fair trial were dim, given the fact that favoritism and discrimination were so widespread.

James went against the generally accepted practice of his day, which gave deference to the wealthy, the well-dressed, and the well-placed—a practice that still continues. It is a natural human tendency to highly esteem the rich and powerful, giving them special consideration, even at the expense of the poor. Alex Moyter reminds us that "it is not all that long ago, indeed, when the wealthy paid an annual rent to secure a well-placed seat in our parish churches, while those who could not raise the financial wind had to be content with seat in the far-off corners bearing the (actual) label 'Free' " (90). Even if such blatant inequality is a thing of the past, money still does a lot of loud talking in church and society. James said then, and it is applicable now, "have you not [by such behavior] discriminated among yourself and become judges with evil thoughts" (2:4).

The Chosen Poor

Having illustrated faulty religion, James now demonstrates how different is God's standard of judgment and His values from those who are "judges with evil thoughts" (vs. 4)—those who court the rich and neglect the poor. These have reversed true divine values. In God's value system, as demonstrated in both the Old and New Testament, the poor are specially chosen to be His elect ones and inheritors of the kingdom. This is the first point James makes (vs. 5). He immediately follows this with the reason why the rich are so obnoxious (vss. 6, 7), so that no one would ever question God's preference for the poor.

We must note that when he makes his first point, James says simply, "the poor *in* the world" (vs. 5). The NIV adds the words, "in the eyes of." This addition spiritualizes the text and takes away the social and economic punch of the passage. James's idea is a spatial one. The poor are existing *in* poverty. He is saying the same thing Jesus articulated in Luke 6:20: "Blessed are you who are poor." Full stop! Period! Luke does not have Jesus adding ". . . in spirit," as does Matthew 5:3). Yet, I have argued elsewhere that Matthew and Luke are in agreement. I believe that in Matthew the primary sense of the text is spatial. The poor *in spirit* are the materially poor who are in the spiritual community, that is, the church. This parallels the exact phrase found in the Qumran community documents (found in 1948 by the Dead Sea)—a community that existed during the first century. The "poor in spirit" at Qumran were members who lived communally in a religious setting and were poor economically (Maynard-Reid, "Poor and Rich," 179). James, of course, does not mention here the church or some limited community; he speaks more in general terms of the poor in the world who are suffering.

The point of verse 5 is not so much the economic situation that the poor are currently experiencing but the purpose for which they are chosen—not so much their present suffering, but the promised hope. They are chosen to be rich in the sphere of faith (i.e., in that special relationship of trust with God) and inheritors of God's promised kingdom.

This passage, particularly 2:5, is problematic for many Christians, because it seems to exclude the wealthy from both the experience of faith and final salvation. And if we read James carefully, we will find that is exactly what he meant. For him, the rich were outside the sphere of faith and salvation. As was noted earlier, James shows affinity with Luke, who pronounces blessings on the poor but woes on the rich (Luke 6:20, 24). For James, piety does not belong *more* to the poor than to the rich. Piety belongs *only* to the poor. The idea that the wealthy were specially blessed by God and that the poor were cursed because of their laziness is foreign to the theology of this epistle—as well as to the theology of Jesus and Luke.

But James doesn't just make a blanket statement that the poor are chosen and imply that the rich are rejected and leave it at that. He immediately gives reasons why the rich are outside the sphere of faith and salvation. Three reasons are given in 2:6, 7. The rich: (1) exploit; (2) drag the less fortunate into court; and (3) slander God's name.

The exploitation and oppression mentioned in our text take exactly the same forms as that which was done to the poor, strangers, orphans, and widows in Old Testament times, which the ancient prophets readily denounced (Jer. 7:6; 22:3; Ezek. 18:12; Amos 4:1; 8:4; Mal. 3:5; compare Wisdom of Solomon 2:10). The term James uses for exploitation in 2:6 has violent overtones with emphasis on domination. Interestingly, the one other place in which this word is used in the New Testament pictures the devil as the oppressor (Acts 10:38)!

Physical exploitation involved the rich taking legal action against the poor. Legal action over matters such as debts, rents, wages, and pledges seems to be at issue here, and the subjects of the denunciation are the big financiers or bankers. The dragging of debtors into court was intensified because Jewish teachers and leaders had nullified God's command that during the sabbatical year all debts should be canceled (Deut. 15:8). The courts were thus used as a forum for economic oppression, not unlike the judicial system of today. Simon Kistemaker notes that in modern times it is the rich who "are able to afford the help of lawyers to press a claim or file a suit. Check the records in the court and the evidence will show that, generally, not the poor but the rich bring suit against others" (*James*, 79).

The ultimate reason for the rejection of the wealthy is their slandering of God's name. The "noble name" mentioned in 2:7 is the very special name for God in the Old Testament—Yahweh. So holy was this name the Jews never pronounced it, and special care and reverence were taken when the word was written. People and places called by Yahweh's name were His special property. James is saying, then, that the poor who are chosen by God are His special property (vs. 5). To exploit and oppress them is to slander their Owner. This is similar to the words of the ancient sage who said, "He who mocks the poor shows contempt for their Maker" (Prov. 17:5). Oppression and exploitation of, and discrimination against, the poor are clearly an insult to God. James calls it slander, blasphemy!

The Eleventh Commandment

James 2:8 may be understood as suggesting that James's readers, whom he is reproving, are justifying their attention to the wealthy by quoting the command, "Love your neighbor as yourself." Yet from the previous verses it is clear they are showing favoritism. They are using this ancient command to love one's neighbor as an excuse to show partiality to the rich, arguing that they are simply doing neighborly, loving deeds. James says that showing love to a neighbor is good but showing partiality is bad.

It is interesting that the command to love one's neighbor is taken from Leviticus 19:18, where the very context indicates the problem of showing partiality—either to the poor or the rich. In Leviticus 19:15, only three verses earlier, God commands Israel, "Do not pervert justice. Do not show partiality to the poor or favoritism to the great, but judge your neighbor fairly." According to what God says in Leviticus, if we favor one group over another—rich or poor—we have not shown love to our neighbor.

James's reaction to such discrimination demonstrates that it is not a small thing. It is not simply a little weakness of character—a natural tendency we all have in an evil world. Favoritism to the rich, in James's book, is more than a small flaw; it is sin. He addresses his readers strongly: "If you show favoritism, you sin and are convicted by the law as lawbreakers" (2:9).

The fact that James makes his prohibition against partiality to the rich at the expense of the poor a kind of "eleventh" commandment shows how serious he considers showing favoritism to be. When we read verse 10 ("For whoever keeps the whole law and yet stumbles at just one point is guilty of breaking all of it"), in context, we cannot but agree that the "one point" he refers to here is showing favoritism. Although many evangelists have used this as a key text for seventh-day Sabbath keeping, this is not James's point at all! Yet, with the same intensity that we Adventists have shown for upholding the fourth commandment, James denounces those who break his "eleventh" commandment.

One may object that James does not intend to elevate the command against favoritism to the level of the ten moral words in Exodus 20 or Deuteronomy 5. I would disagree, and 2:11 demonstrates that James also disagrees. In verse 11 he selects two of the most heinous sins listed in the Ten Commandments to place in parallel with "favoritism." He writes: "For he who said, 'Do not commit adultery,' also said, 'Do not murder.' If you do not commit adultery but do commit murder, you have become a lawbreaker" (vs. 11). "Lawbreaker" is the very word he used in verse 9 in reference to the person showing favoritism to the rich! James has murder, adultery, and favoritism all on an equal plane!

Although no other New Testament author is as strident as James in his denunciation of favoritism, we cannot deny that all New Testament writers saw discrimination as a serious sin. Paul, in Galatians 3:28, argues "there is neither Jew nor Greek, slave nor free, male nor female, for you are all one in Christ." And even more clear is the message in Colossians 3:11 where Paul shows that the barriers between Jews and Greeks, circumcised and uncircumcised, barbarian and Scythian, slave and free are all broken down (compare Eph. 2:11-22). There can be no discrimination as far as nationality, race, ethnic background, class, gender, religion, etc. are concerned.

This teaching has as much relevance to us today as it had in the days of James and Paul. The continuing problem of race relations in the United States (African-Americans versus Caucasian-Americans or Jewish-Americans; Hispanic, Latino, or Chicano-Americans versus Americans of European heritage), as well as the subtle, and sometimes overt, discrimination (even within some homogeneous groups), is abominable in God's sight. Just as obnoxious is the classism to be found in places such as Jamaica, where the person with lighter-colored skin ("brown skin") is favored over the individual with darker skin ("black skin"). James would also have come down just as hard on the racism in Trinidad between the Negroid and Indian people, or in Rwanda between the Hutu and the Tutsi, or the French-speaking and English-speaking peoples of Quebec, Canada. For James, partiality shown to any of these groups at the expense of the other is sin, and the perpetrator of the act is convicted by the law as a lawbreaker (2:9)!

The fate of the lawbreaker is certain—"judgment without mercy" (vs. 13). James is here pointing a critical finger at those who have not shown mercy to the poor and is predicting that the tables will be turned on them. This verse echoes the negative side of the positive beatitude of Matthew 5:7, "Blessed are the merciful, for they will be shown mercy." According to James, those who fail to demonstrate a merciful care to the poor should not expect mercy and compassion from God.

Jesus' teaching in the Gospels emphasized the characteristic trait of God that freely grants mercy to those who desire it and request it. On the other hand, the person who fails to extend mercy and compassion to a fellow human being can expect only judgment without mercy. This point is highlighted in the parable of the king who forgave the debtor servant, yet the latter refused to show mercy to a fellow debtor who found it difficult to pay (Matt. 18:23-35). Jesus ended the parable with the words: " 'Then the master called the [first] servant in. "You wicked servant," he said, "I canceled all that debt of yours because you begged me to. Shouldn't you have had mercy on your fellow servant just as I had on you?" In anger his master turned him over to the jailers until he should pay back all he owed' " (Matt. 18:32-34).

James, in the same manner, has God meting out judgment upon the unmerciful lawbreaker who shows partiality to the rich. But God's desire is that "mercy triumphs over judgment" (2:13). God's call through James is for mercy and justice for the poor (and marginal) to replace favoritism to the rich and powerful. Like Micah, James would say, "He has showed you, O man, what is good, and what does the Lord require of you? To act justly and *to love mercy* and to walk humbly with your God" (Micah 6:8).

■ Getting Into the Word

James 2:14-26

Before doing the following exercises, read James 1:27–2:26 again; then carefully read 2:14-26 two or three times.

1. **Prior to your careful reading of James, how did you interpret "works" in this epistle? Why?**
2. **Read Romans 4:1-24. Does this chapter contradict James 2:14-26? (Especially compare and contrast Romans 4:2, 3 with James 2:21-23; also Romans 3:28 with James 2:24.) Explain your answer.**
3. **Some interpret faith and works as referring to the theological concepts of justification and sanctification, respectively. Do you agree? Explain. If you don't agree, demonstrate from James what the use of these terms mean in context.**

■ Exploring the Word

Faith and Works: the Debate

The issue of faith and works from James's perspective has been debated at two levels: at the level of those to whom he is writing, and at the level of later interpreters of the epistle. We cannot understand the text without hearing the various voices participating in the debate, while at the same time listening without prejudice to what James is saying within his context.

Due to the controversial nature of James 2:14-26, many have argued that these verses are the most important contribution of the apostle to New Testament theology. It is even suggested that the passage is at the theological heart of the letter. Yet, it seems to me that such a conclusion can be drawn only externally and not by a careful, internal analysis of the epistle. In other words, this passage takes on a super-life if it is pitted against the writings of Paul in which the issue of faith and works is dominant. When the passage is read in its immediate context, however, it suddenly becomes not the theological heart of James's letter but rather an illustration of the larger point he is making in the section beginning with 1:27.

We do injustice to James's argument when we make a clear dichotomy between the discussion in the verses preceding 2:14 and that of the subsequent verses. We should not, for example, read verse 13 apart from verse 14. The merciful person is the very person who operates out of an unbroken faith-works paradigm. The individual of faith is the individual whose works are merciful.

If the connection between verses 13 and 14 is not clearly seen, the connection between verses 2, 3 and verses 15, 16 cannot be ignored. The treatment of the person in shabby clothing in verse 3 and the individual without food and clothes in verses 15, 16 are echoes of the same concern. And the treatment of each stands in stark parallelism as is clearly seen in verses 3 and 16. The presentation of both these illustrations at the beginning of verses 1-13 and verses 14-26 indicates that concern for the poor is at the heart of James's concern here. In reality, the illustrations and the discussions that follow are but a continuation of the thesis statement made in 1:27: True religion is caring for the suffering poor and the marginal individuals in society.

In order to arouse and challenge his readers to practice and live a religion that is not grounded in dead faith but that has its roots in practical social outreach, James engages in a debate with an imaginary opponent. The literary style he employs is a Greek rhetorical device called the "diatribe." In the lively discussion in which this device is used, James has an objector put forth his or her own viewpoint as a foil for James's position. This is clearly illustrated in 2:18: "But someone will say, 'You have faith; I have deeds.' Show me your faith without deeds, and I will show you my faith by what I do." In verse 14 he makes this point by asking two rhetorical questions: "What good is it, my brothers, if a man claims to have faith but has no deeds? Can such a faith save him?" Both questions are constructed with the Greek negative particle *mē*, which requires a negative answer. James makes it plain: Faith without deeds is not salvific.

This theological position of James has led interpreters as far back as Martin Luther to argue forcefully that James is in conflict with Paul because the latter presents the exact opposite viewpoint. Such interpreters note, for example, that a comparison of James 2:14-26 and Romans 3:28–4:24 discloses a distinct similarity in the choice of words, the combination of words and phrases, and even the Old Testament quotation chosen (Gen. 15:6). Because there are so many similarities between these passages from Paul and James, yet such stark opposing conclusions, it is proposed by some that James wrote to criticize Paul. Others argue that Paul (who wrote after James) wanted to present a better understanding of the significance of faith without works.

To have Paul and James in opposition is to misunderstand each author. They are not engaging each other; they are not involved in a debate. They are combating quite opposite problems. Joachim Jeremias accurately notes that the "field of battle is different"—the "zone of conflict" each author is occupying is distinct ("Paul and James," 370; Longenecker, 207). Each writer develops the same words, phrases, and quotations "from his own perspective and for his own purpose" (Kistemaker, "The Theological Message," 60). They write independently of each other and approach the subject differently. As was noted earlier in the Introduction, one approaches it theologically and the other ethically.

Sophie Laws supports this contention when she notes that if James were actually debating Paul in this passage, he most likely would not pass over Paul's linkage of Genesis 15:6 with the account of Abraham's circumcision in chapter 18. Instead, James link chapter 15 with chapter 22 and the offering of Isaac. If Paul, on the other hand, were truly debating James, he would address James's reference to the case of Rahab. But we find no mention of Rahab in the Pauline argument (129). It is important, as Leon Morris says, "not to be hypnotized by words" (83) but rather to listen to what each author means in his own context. Let's illustrate.

Paul's doctrine of justification by faith grew out of the conflict he had in his early ministry with judaizing Christians who sought to save themselves by the observance of law, particularly their insistence on circumcision. Paul's concern, thus, can be understood only in light of this polemic with these legalistic Christians. With this in mind, when Paul uses the word *works* in the context of legalism, it must be interpreted as "works of law" (a phrase he himself uses in the Greek in such places as Rom. 3:28)—what scholars call "nomistic religion," or an attempt to earn salvation by keeping the law (whether it be the moral or the ceremonial law). On the other hand, because James's polemic is different, when he employs the term *works*, he has in mind deeds of mercy and compassion.

This debate over whether James and Paul are in conflict will remain alive as long as biblical interpreters read the text of James through the lens of Paul. But each author must be read through his own spectacles. "We should try to be discerning exegetes," says Thorwald Lorenzen, "by being servants of the text, not masters over it. We must try to listen, before we speak" (231).

One other important interpretive point should be made here. Let us remember that neither James nor Paul were systematic theologians, writing out their theological reflections from ivory-tower studies. They were not developing what theologians call full-blown soteriologies—the study of salvation. They were pastors and leaders who simply addressed limited concerns (even though the address was vigorous). The question, therefore, as to whether the Bible (or the writings of James and Paul) contradicts itself is a wrong question. We need to allow each author under the influence of the Holy Spirit to address different issues and different situations in diverse and even in seemingly contradictory ways. If we can bring ourselves to allow this, then we will not be disturbed by the fact that theological and ethical statements are many times conditioned by the historical settings. James's and Paul's discussion on faith and works is such a case in point.

In the debate James is having with his imaginary opponent (2:14-26), he makes it clear that a faith that lacks deeds cannot save (1:14). A question that arises at this point is: What is this "faith" that James makes reference to? We must first note that James does not define faith. The meaning of the concept can be determined or surmised only by the context. But in James the context is not always clear (except for 2:19, which has been traditionally understood as referring to faith as intellectual assent by the demons). This latter definition of faith as intellectual assent to a body of facts or truth has been imposed upon the rest of James, and thus faith in the epistle is determined to be confession of doctrine, assent to correct beliefs or cognitive acceptance of Jesus as Saviour. We will see, however, that this definition is narrow even for verse 19. It seems that James is using faith much more broadly.

Although our author does not define the term, I believe he is using the "faith" concept to indicate one's trust in God. James sees faith more in terms of relationship than in terms of proposition. For him, it has to do with attitude; it is practical. James is not attacking this practical faith. What he opposes is those who verbalize the idea that they have faith but who do not really understand what they are talking about. Genuine faith, being practical, does not exist without external expression. It is a fallacy to conceive of a relationship that lacks action—one that is deedless. James is thus contrasting a false faith with genuine faith.

That James is making a contrast between a genuine and false faith is demonstrated in the final phrase of verse 14 where he says, "Can *such* faith save him?" The King James Version's translation of this phrase confuses the point. It reads, "Can faith save him?" But James is not arguing whether faith saves or not; he is clearly stating that the mere verbalized idea of faith by his opponent has no salvific power.

It is interesting that the idea of salvation comes immediately after verse 13, which speaks about judgment. The juxtaposing of salvation and judgment indicates James is dealing with one issue. The point he is making is that those who fail to demonstrate a true faith can expect only damnation and judgment, not mercy and salvation. His call, therefore, is for a practice of true faith, one that works through love (to use Paul's expression in Gal. 5:6). This is the only faith that is salvific and not dead and barren.

It is important as we read James that we hold his message in tension with Paul's and do not attempt to impose one upon the other.

In attempts to systematize the Scriptures, in this case the writings of both apostles, many have argued that James and Paul are dealing with faith as manifested at two different periods of the individual's life. They say that in the case of Paul, when he speaks of salvation or justification, he is talking about *preconversion* faith, or the initial step a person makes in his or her relationship with Christ. In James's case, on the other hand, they suggest that he is presenting a theology of sanctification—the life that must be lived *after* justification if one desires to be saved. Is such a harmony correct, however? Or is this only an attempt to have James and Paul saying the same thing and voicing the same concerns?

Instead of making a parallel between James and Paul, what if we compared James with John the Baptist? In John's call to repentance, he told the crowds coming to him to "produce fruit in keeping with repentance" (Matt. 3:8; Luke 3:8). In Luke's record of the narrative, it is clear that John's call to repentance included social concern—sharing the clothes and food with those who had none, not collecting more taxes than is required, and giving up extortion totally (Luke 3:10-14). All this is prior to baptism! Amazingly, the illustrations given in Luke mirror the illustrations in James 2.

The problem we face as we read the New Testament is a Western one—the need to have a clear-cut order of salvation (what theologians call *ordo salutis*). But the Scriptures have no such interest. A total reading of the New Testament demonstrates that there is no one specific order in which the experience of salvation must take place. What we find instead is that salvation is inclusive. The context and pastoral concerns of the individual Bible writer dictates which aspect of this simple, yet complex, concept is emphasized. For James, genuine faith and works are complementary and concurrent. Both are essential in the salvation event.

Faith and Works Illustrated

Immediately after James makes his thesis statement—that false faith (which lacks deeds) does not save—he illustrates his point by stating what genuine faith is like. This he does in 2:15-17, in which social concern is highlighted. We will return to this later.

The objector is not at all satisfied with James's position. For James's opponent, faith and works are "two distinguishable, unconnected items" (McKnight, 362). Thus the objection is raised: "you have faith; I have deeds." In the opinion of this interlocutor, faith and works are separate things in the spiritual life. But James challenges the speaker to demonstrate this unconnectedness. James says, "Show me your faith without deeds, and I will show you my faith by what I do" (vs. 18). This is an impossible challenge to meet as far as James is concerned. To be demonstrated, faith must be visible and tangible. Faith, therefore, is impossible to show apart from works. In James's context, true faith is demonstrable, and for that reason it is impossible to separate it from action. To make his point, he presents three illustrations: demons, Abraham, and Rahab.

In his first illustration, James shatters the confidence of those who think that faith alone is of value—just as Jesus did when He said in the Sermon on the Mount, " 'Not everyone who says to me, "Lord, Lord," will enter the kingdom of heaven, but only he who does the will of my Father who is in heaven' " (Matt. 7:21). Here James, just as poignantly, says to his opponent, "You believe that there is one God. Good! Even the demons believe that—and shudder" (2:19).

James may be using irony when he says *even* the demons believe in the unity of God. Ralph Martin has rightly noted that "to believe that God is one is indeed necessary, but not sufficient, for even the demons believe, though no one in James's audience would admit that such faith is able to save them." This simply indicates, says Martin, "that the demons react to the divine *numen*. . . . But even with this admission, there is little that can be said for this type of faith: it is worse than useless" (89).

We must here grasp the point, as Sophie Laws has well stated, that James "is not concerned to contrast faith, as intellectual assent, with works, but to indicate the necessary outcome of faith, if it is a live faith, and the impossibility of it existing alone. For the demons, belief in the God who is one produces a response of fear" (128). The question for the objector is, "Is your faith whole enough that your response is different from that of the demons, whose response is one of *shuddering* [a verb used in ancient magical texts for the effects of exorcism]?" Or "Is your faith one in which positive social action is clearly demonstrated?" For James, the issue in this illustration is: What is the response of faith? It is impossible for faith to exist in a vacuum. The response—the demonstration—will identify faith as either genuine or demonic.

James realizes that his opponent has not grasped the point with the little illustration about demons. So he becomes even more forceful and addresses the imaginary person with blunt, uncomplimentary language. "You foolish man," he says (vs. 20; The New American Bible translates the phrase "you ignoramus!"). Such a person is literally an empty head, inane, and deficient in understanding. Then James asks, "Do you want evidence that faith without deeds is useless?" (vs. 20). Here, there is a play on words. "Useless" literally means "without work" (*a* + *ergos* in Greek; *a* being a particle of negation). So James is saying here that faith that has no works (*ergos*) does not work (*argos*). The objector is so dumb he or she cannot comprehend this point. James has to supply more evidence. He sets forth then to illustrate what he is saying by two figures popular in Jewish history and folklore. They are contrasting individuals—one is a holy patriarch and founder of the Hebrew people; the other is a *sinful, foreign*, woman. But both illustrate in their lives and actions that faith and deeds cannot be disjointed.

The reason James uses Abraham as one of his major examples is possibly because the objector had put Abraham forth as a classic example of faith that needs no works. The objector, like Paul in his Romans' context (see Rom. 4:22), most likely was using Genesis 15:6 to argue that faith alone is essential; because all Abraham did was believe, and it was credited to him as righteousness. James disagrees with that interpretation. The question James poses demands a Yes (based on the Greek text formulation of the question) and so demonstrates that Abraham was justified, or considered righteous, by what he *did*. James asked: "Was not our ancestor Abraham considered righteous for what he did when he offered his son Isaac on the altar?" (2:21).

It is James's use of the word *dikaioō* (justify, consider righteous) that has caused the theological storm in the interpretation of this passage. Paul makes it clear (Rom. 4) that a person is *not* justified by works but by faith alone and that Abraham's story proves it. James says the opposite—and cites Abraham's story to prove it! Who is right? Who is wrong? Since Luther, James has been judged wrong because his use of the term *dikaioō* contradicts the forensic, legal definition given to it by Protestant interpreters. This definition refers to that initial act of God in which the sinner is considered righteous (justified) when he or she accepts Jesus Christ as Saviour and Lord.

The fact is, however, that James has no such forensic, legal interpretation of justification in mind. As a matter of fact, it is doubtful that even Paul intended the concept to be defined thus. More and more, biblical scholars are coming to affirm that both Paul's and James's use of the term is very Hebraic; that is, both used it in the Old Testament sense of a covenant relationship. In Paul's polemic against the legalistic judaizers, whose focus was on keeping the letter of the law in order to be saved, he wished to focus on the believer's initial entrance into that relationship. James, however, is dealing with the ethics of concern for the poor and marginal and has an interest that is more wholistic. Of the two apostles, James is closer to the Old Testament understanding of justification as a covenant relationship combined with fidelity and obedience.

It is important to note that James is not putting together a chronological sequence of justification. We are, therefore, wrong to propose that Paul's justification is the initial declaration of righteousness, while James's is the final, eschatological verdict after the Christian has proved to be righteous by the good deeds performed or the keeping of the commandments perfectly. The fact is that even though James illustrates his point with a single incident in Abraham's life (the offering of Isaac—Gen. 22), his use of Genesis 15:6 in verse 24 should not be limited to that one incident. The experience of justification includes Abraham's entire lifetime; the incident on Mount Moriah with Isaac is only a part of it. That this is so is confirmed by the Greek imperfect tense in 2:22, where James says "you see that his faith and his actions *were working together (sunērgei)*."

The imperfect tense indicates a continuous, ongoing activity. Faith, works, justification, covenant relationship, and fidelity run together continuously in Abraham's life. Because of this wholistic relationship, Abraham is elevated to the status of being called "God's friend" (vs. 23).

James has made his point from Abraham's life. He can now conclude with the dogmatic assertion that "a person is justified by what he does and not by faith *alone*" (vs. 24). It is ironic, as Sophie Laws has noted, that it is James, not Paul, who gave Luther the term "by faith alone" (137). Paul does not use the word *alone* in his Greek text. But Luther felt it should be there and inserted it in his German text—and then used it against James! But James's theology does not exclude faith or works. The fact that he uses the word *alone* is an indication that he does not wish to discard faith. His ethics and his theology include both faith and works.

With verse 24, one would think that James has hit the bull's eye; he has scored the ultimate point. Yet he seems to feel that his argument is not complete. So he gives one final illustration. It is an illustration of hospitality that is exactly the opposite of the story at the beginning of the chapter (vss. 2, 3). The positioning of these two hospitality illustrations is another strong evidence that the entire chapter 2 of James should be read as a unit.

After illustrating his point with a patriarch, James chooses a foreign woman who was traditionally thought to be a prostitute to demonstrate that she was justified *on the basis of what she did*. Rahab is an example from the bottom of the social ladder. Although her initial vocation was less than honorable, she became a heroine in Jewish folk legend. Rahab, Sarah, Abigail, and Esther were the four chief Israelite beauties. Rabbinic traditions tell of Rahab marrying Joshua and becoming the ancestress of eight priests who were also prophets; most notable among them were Jeremiah and Ezekiel. She herself was a prophetess, tradition has it! Interestingly, in the Matthean genealogy (Matt. 1:2-16) Rahab is singled out with three other women (Tamar, Ruth, and Bathsheba) as an ancestress of Christ. It is significant that all four women's sexual unions were, initially at least, irregular or questionable and thus served as types of Mary (Laws, 137). It is this type of person that James chooses for his final illustration.

Rahab is justified, or considered righteous, for what she did. In Joshua 2:2-21 her action was protecting the spies from the king, giving them a place to sleep for the night, and sending them to the hills the next morning. James's telling of the story adds that she sent them another way (2:25). But his emphasis, as is that of Joshua, is on the fact that she showed hospitality to the spies. This is exactly what James means by faith that works. Faith without social action is an oxymoron. It is impossible. "As the body without the spirit is dead, so faith without deeds is dead" (vs. 26).

Faith and Works: The Main Problem

Too often, interpreters of this passage (vss. 14-26) focus on the illustrations of the demons, Abraham, or Rahab (especially Abraham), or on the debate as to whether James or Paul is theologically correct. These foci miss the main problem of James. This problem is stated first, even before the illustrations. Yet it is ignored by Bible students. It is important that the faithful interpreter of the text listen to the emphasis of the author and not impose his or her own concerns on the passage, making them the primary intent of the text.

The main problem in this passage is found in verses 15-17, what some might call "a little parable." "Suppose a brother or sister is without clothes and daily food. If one of you says to him, 'Go, I wish you well; keep warm and well fed,' but does nothing about his physical needs, what good is it? In the same way, faith by itself, if it is not accompanied by action, is dead" (vss. 15-17). This incident, far from being a fictional parable, was a real-life situation in James's community. A careful reading of the epistle, and insights from the social history of the time and the geographical setting of James, reveals that poverty was an enduring state for much of his audience. What is so sad is that even within his community there were those who ignored even the basic needs of their neighbors, while elevating their own so-called faith as more important. James is precise: such a faith is dead; such a religion is unacceptable.

Not much has changed since the time of James as far as the attitude of many Christians is concerned. Our focus on personal faith at the exclusion of social action is a plague on Christianity. Sensitivity to the needs of the poor is not reckoned to be an essential ingredient in the Christian's life. Instead, the needy are ignored, or they are told to stop being lazy and better themselves. This reaction is no different from the reaction in James. Simon Kistemaker makes this point well: "The remark *Go, I wish you well* [is] summarized in the popular saying *God helps those who help themselves*. That is, let the shivering, hungry brother or sister pull themselves up by their own bootstraps. 'Keep warm and well fed.' If the poverty-stricken brother or sister would only exert themselves, they would have plenty to eat and sufficient clothing to wear. And God would bless them" (*James*, 89). If James were writing today, he would challenge such a reaction. He would agree with former United States Supreme Court Justice Thurgood Marshall, who said that nobody ever pulled himself or herself up by his or her own bootstraps. I am convinced that each of us is what we are because someone else stuck out a helping hand. I believe also that James would disagree with Benjamin Franklin's statement (often quoted as a biblical statement!) that God helps those who help themselves. The biblical truth is that God helps me to help others, particularly those in need.

James's message is not only for the individual but for the body of believers—the church. Too often our focus is almost exclusively on the so-called "spiritual" needs of the church or the individual. The proclamation of the gospel is centered on church growth and personal salvation to the exclusion of the bodily needs of society and the individual. Again, Kistemaker notes that "at times, Christians proclaim the gospel of the Lord without any regard for the physical needs of their hearers. They tell the people about salvation, but they seem to forget that poverty-stricken people need clothes and food to make the gospel relevant. Unless word and deed go together, unless preaching of the gospel is accompanied by a program of social action, unless faith is demonstrated in loving care and concern, faith is dead" (*James*, 89).

I like how the *Clear Word* paraphrase of James's illustration mirrors the way in which many genuine Christians react to those in need: "When brothers and sisters in need of clothing and food come to you for help, you say to them, 'We're so sorry. We will certainly pray for you. Keep warm and fed, and may the God of peace be with you,' but you don't do anything for them, what good is your statement of faith?" (2:15, 16). James states that this faith, this religion, is dead, ineffectual, useless, and totally unacceptable before God. Faith and "religion that God our Father accepts as pure and faultless is this: to look after orphans and widows in their distress and to keep oneself from being polluted by the world" (1:27).

■ Applying the Word

James 1:27–2:26

1. Do I tend to emphasize the vertical, personal aspect of religion ("keeping myself from being polluted by the world") while ignoring the horizontal, social dimension ("look after orphans and widows")? In what ways can I make them equally important?
2. What specific social activities could I participate in that would demonstrate true religion in my community? List them.
3. In what specific ways have I found myself to be partial to persons who least need my partiality? During the last twelve months, who was I more partial to when I had the opportunity to give presents on special days (birthdays, graduations, Christmas, Three Kings Day)? Was it those who had or was it those in need? List the recipients in two columns: the haves and the have-nots. If I had to live the last year over, after having read James, how would the list be different?
4. Do I find myself being unnecessarily extravagant in my dress and in the other things I possess? Do I sometimes criticize a person with an inexpensive wedding band, yet I drive a top-of-the-line import vehicle; my house is filled with the finest expensive objects; my closets overflowing with high-priced dresses, suits, and footwear? How specifically can I change

my attitude and lifestyle to bring it in line with the message
of James?

5. Am I overly critical of the large church growth occurring in
the underdeveloped societies of two-thirds of the world or
in poor segments of societies in the developed world? Is it
possible these poor converts are attracted to the gospel and
the community of faith because they are "rich in faith"? Discuss.

6. Do I tend to have a hierarchy of sins; for example, adultery
and assassination at the top, and pride and partiality at the
bottom? (Make a list of sins from worst to least-serious based
on how you have prioritized sins in the past.) How would I
make that list different now?

7. Are there tendencies in my local church that parallel the
description of James's audience in chapter 2 of his epistle?
Does his teaching also have application in the wider society
of my home, community, workplace, school, etc.? Explain.

8. As I consider the priorities of my local church, which of the
following three areas should receive the largest portion of
budgeted funds: (1) social action; (2) public evangelistic outreach; (3) worship and liturgy? If my church had $100 to
spend in those three areas, how would I divide it?

9. How far am I willing to take risky, uncomfortable, and incon-
venient steps to getting to know poor and homeless people?
Am I willing to be incarnated with them by spending time with
them on the streets, in shelters, in their poor hovels—becoming
their friend; while at the same time taking steps to lift them up
out of their poverty-stricken state? Explain in one paragraph
why or why not you should engage in such activities and/or
how much risk you are willing to take.

■ Researching the Word

1. Look up *widows* and *orphans* in your concordance. Write a
paragraph describing their situation. What special regula-
tions did God give regarding their welfare? Did you find

anything special or significant about how they should be treated? Compare your findings with those in a Bible dictionary.

2. Look up the words *faith* and *works* in a Bible dictionary. Summarize the dictionary's definition of each. Do each of these definitions agree with James's definition in his context? Explain how they agree or why they don't agree.

■ Further Study of the Word

1. For a commentary that draws excellent contemporary applications and challenges the reader with the social implications of this passage in today's church and society, see S. J. Kistemaker, *James and I-III John.*

2. For an article that not only does an exegetical study of James 2:1-13 but lays out hermeneutical and homiletical implications for a particular setting (in this case, South Africa), see D. J. Smit, "Exegesis and Proclamation: 'Show no Partiality . . .' (James 2:1-13)."

3. See P. Maynard-Reid, *Poverty and Wealth in James*, for a detailed study of James 2:1-13. Especially see chapter 4, "Favoritism and the Poor," 48-67.

4. For a groundbreaking, seminal study on the debate of faith and works in James, see Joachim Jeremias, "Paul and James."

5. See R. P. Martin's commentary on *James*, which devotes one-eighth of its space to a fairly thorough treatment of the perplexing issue of faith and works. Martin does a good job of interpreting the passage in its immediate textual context.

6. For an extensive study on the concept of "faith" in this epistle, see J. F. MacArthur, Jr., "Faith According to the Apostle James."

PART THREE

James 3:1-18

True
Wisdom

CHAPTER SIX

Proverbs on the Tongue

James 3:1-12

Sticks and stones may break my bones,
but words will never hurt me.

James challenges and reverses this popular childhood taunt. In many instances, the wounds caused by words are more intense and long lasting than those inflicted by sticks and stones. The latter wounds may heal quickly, but often the suffering brought about by the misuse of the tongue never heals.

James does not make it explicitly clear why he spends so much time discussing the tongue. (The tongue and speech is mentioned in every chapter— 1:19, 26; 2:12; 3:1-12; 4:11; 5:12.) But the fact that misused speech is the cause of endless suffering may be the key to our understanding of James's deep concern. In James's most extended exposition on the subject (3:1-12), he discusses it in the context of wisdom. In Hebrew wisdom tradition, wisdom is required to make sense of life's perplexities, and there is a constant interrelation of suffering and wisdom. A careful reading of Proverbs and other Old Testament and Jewish wisdom literature reveals that uncontrolled speech is the cause of much of life's perplexities and sufferings. Here James is possibly using a series of wisdom proverbs to address, from yet another angle, his overall theme of suffering.

It is interesting this major discussion follows the statement that faith without works is dead (2:26). One wonders what is the logical connection. R. V. G. Tasker proposes a solution: "Not unnaturally James follows the statement that faith without works is dead by the reminder that works are

not to be limited to actions. Words are also works. Indeed, much of the work
of the world is accomplished through the medium of words" (72). It seems
doubtful, however, that this is the connection James intends to make.

This discussion of the tongue is more accurately connected to 1:26. In
that verse, James began his presentation of true and faulty religion. There
he stated that "if anyone considers himself religious and yet does not keep a
tight rein on his tongue, he deceives himself and his religion is worthless
(vs. 26). But in the next verse he presents another ingredient of true and
pure religion. Rather than presenting it in the negative, as in verse 26, he
presents it in the positive. In verse 27, the other ingredient of true religion
is concern for the poor and marginal. As James expands his thoughts on
these two aspects of pure religion, he develops the latter (vs. 27) in chapter
2. In chapter 3, he returns to the former (vs. 26) and deals with the problem at length.

■ Getting Into the Word

James 3:1-12

Read the above passage twice and then do the following exercises:

1. In the marginal references of your Bible, note the parallel
   texts from wisdom books (Proverbs, Ecclesiastes, portions
   of Psalms). Look them up and jot them down in your notebook. Browse through these Old Testament books and see
   if you find other passages that speak directly to the issues
   James is addressing in verses 1-12. Make a note of them.
   Can you think of modern proverbs that are similar to James's
   exhortation (for example, "There's many a slip between the
   cup and the lip")? Write them out.
2. List three or four reasons why teachers (or leaders) will be
   judged more strictly than others. Explain each reason.
3. Apart from teaching, are there any other modern profes-
   sions to which James's counsel in verse 1 could apply? List
   them.

4. **In a paragraph, explain how verse 1 relates to the rest of the passage.**
5. **Explain how each of the illustrations and metaphors in the entire passage poignantly and forcefully make James's point.**
6. **How can one praise God and at the same time curse one's fellow human beings? If this is possible, do you think God accepts the praise? Explain.**

■ Exploring the Word

Teachers and Their Tongues

The first admonition in this section (3:1-12) is addressed to teachers. We are not sure of the specific identity of these individuals. The fact that the admonition occurs within a wisdom passage suggests that they might be sages or teachers of wisdom in the community and individual congregations. In the time of James, many of these teachers were rabbis, and many young men eagerly sought this position of privilege and power. The ambition of Jewish parents, as well, was to have their sons trained as rabbis. To be a rabbinic teacher was highly desirable. John A. Burns notes that "any social contact one might have with a rabbi was desirable: whether to speak with him, have him as a house-guest, to marry his daughter—even to carry his burdens, fetch him water, or saddle his donkey" (124; see also Jeremias's enormously helpful study in *Jerusalem in the Time of Jesus*, 233-244, for many illustrations of the high respect accorded to teachers within Judaism). The teachers may not only be rabbis but leaders of synagogues or other types of congregations. James's warnings could possibly have a sociological basis as well. These "teachers" or "wise ones" might be part of the Zealot political network he will address more explicitly in the next chapter. At this point, it is not clear if James has a special group in mind or if he has any group in mind. He could be addressing leaders and teachers in congregations, synagogues, political and social parties, as well as whoever "the shoe fits." What we are sure of is that James includes himself by the use of the first person plural in this opening verse.

But he warns that not many of his audience should presume to be teachers.

The reason for this warning, in the context of his discussion on the tongue, has to be that James recognizes that teachers are persons of words *par excellence*. The very nature of their work exposes them to the danger of their speech offending and causing suffering. Not only are teachers trained to be critical (and are in many instances severely critical) but their prominent position allows them to stimulate their followers to actions that can bring about pain and suffering. Thus both the agent (the teacher) and the instrument (the tongue) can be dangerous.

On the surface, this opening verse seems to be meant to discourage persons from becoming teachers within the community. But that is not James's point. His emphasis is found in the last phrase of the first verse: "because you know that we who teach will be judged more strictly." James is pointing to the dangers inherent in this vocation of awesome responsibility. The greater the responsibility, the greater the judgment. Those who use words as a tool of trade have great responsibility, and the misuse of the instrument will bring on severe judgment. James's words bring to mind Jesus' saying in Matthew 12:36, 37, " 'But I tell you that men will have to give account on the day of judgment for every careless word they have spoken. For by your words you will be acquitted, and by your words you will be condemned.' " If this is true of all persons, how much more is it true of the teacher whose prominent leadership position and eloquence of speech gives him or her enormous power and responsibility?

Before we are too quick to thumb our noses at teachers and use this text as a stick over their heads, let us hear what James has to say next. "We all stumble in many ways" (3:2); that is, we all sin and make mistakes. We are all vulnerable. None can say that he or she has not erred, because all have at least one sin in common—the misuse of the tongue. But the sign of a mature person is the ability to control his or her tongue. This is the point of the latter part of the verse: "If anyone is never at fault in what he says, he is a perfect man, able to keep his whole body in check" (vs. 2).

As we noted earlier in our discussion of 1:4, the definition of a perfect person is not one who makes no mistakes—not one who is sinless. Rather, the emphasis is on maturity and wholeness. James Adamson, in commenting on this verse, notes: "The Greek *teleios* [perfect] in its original sense contains the . . . notion of progress from an immature, unripe, inchoate state to a perfect mature, ripe, complete, and completing 'finish' or *telos*—where *telos* signifies not just where something stops but where it has attained the consummated fullness of growth or progress in the attributes and qualities that lie with the nature of its species" (*James: The Man*, 369, 370). Even though this is the basic meaning of perfection, James seems to have a higher standard, suggesting that if one never makes a mistake in what he or she says, that one is perfect. James does not say, however, that such a state is, or is not, attainable in this life. What he does admit is that we all stumble and that the tongue is the source of much of the tripping up. Thus, if we could somehow have some control over that member of the body, the possibility of keeping the whole person in check would be greater.

Let us note here that James is not alone in his intense interest in the power of the tongue. There is much written in earlier wisdom literature regarding the same. The book of Proverbs, particularly, has much to say concerning the unruly and hasty tongue versus the controlled tongue. For example. Proverbs 10:19 states: "When words are many, sin is not absent, but he who holds his tongue is wise" (compare 10:8, 11; 16:27, 28; 18:7, 8). But it is in James's seemingly favorite apocryphal wisdom book that we find a text that parallels his, highlighting the idea that we all stumble with our tongue. In this text, Jesus ben Sirach writes, "A person may make a slip without intending it. Who has not sinned with his tongue?" (Sir. 19:16, NRSV). William Barclay notes that of all Jewish writers, Sirach "was most impressed with the terrifying potentialities of the tongue" (82). (See, for example, 5:13–6:1; 14:1; 19:15; 22:27; and especially 28:13–26.)

Horse's Bit

James wants his audience to grasp the magnitude of his argument that the tongue is powerful and dangerous. Though it is small in size, he argues, it is great in its achievement. In order to forcefully make this point, he presents a series of illustrations: the small bit that controls the big horse, the small rudder that steers the large ship even in a storm; the small spark that sets a great forest on fire; and the fact that all animals and creatures can be tamed (3:3-8). None of these illustrations are original to James. He draws the images in the world of his audience to make his point.

The first in the series of metaphors focuses on the small bit in the horse's mouth (vs. 5). Even though the size of the bit is not expressly stated, the mention of "the whole animal" at the end of the verse is intended to highlight the smallness of the guiding instrument and the greatness of its effect. Anyone who is familiar with horses will confirm that if a horse is not broken to the bridle and bit while it is young, that animal will run and gallop with misdirected energy. But if the animal is broken and the bit is accepted, the largest of horses will be at the mercy of the rider.

The simile and analogy are impressive but not exactly parallel. For as Duane Watson has pointed out, the bridle controls the horse, "but the tongue does not control the person in quite the same physical manner." However, he notes, "on a broader level, the point of comparison is that a smaller element of a larger whole can greatly impact the direction of the larger whole" (58). The tongue, though as small as the bit, can achieve great things and has enormous impact upon the whole person, negatively as well as positively.

Ship's Rudder

This idea of the small object being able to affect and control a larger one is reinforced in the second illustration (vs. 4). As in the case of the bit and the horse, James chooses another illustration with which his audience was quite familiar. Horses over land and ships by sea were the two popular modes of transportation. Of course, ships then were not as large as our modern ocean liners and cruise vessels, but they did seem large to people of the first-century world. We can recall Luke's mention of the Alexandrian ship with its grain cargo and 276 persons, including Paul, bound for Rome (Acts 27:37, 38). Even a vessel this size is enormously large in comparison with the rudder that steers it. It is this small instrument that is one of the most (if not the most) vital objects of the ship in determining the destiny of the vessel, its occupants, and cargo.

In like manner, the tongue, though a small part of the body, is superpowerful in comparison to its size. James says it "makes great boasts" (3:5). His words bring to mind those of the psalmist who wrote, "Their mouths lay claim to heaven, and their tongues take possession of the earth" (Ps. 73:9). Of course, we must admit that James 3:5 does not specifically spell out the idea of arrogance in the boasting of the tongue. This has led R. V. G. Tasker to note that "there is a sense in which the tongue can be said to possess great things of which it can *legitimately* boast. History affords numerous illustrations of the power of great oratory to encourage the depressed, to rouse the careless, to stir men and women to noble action, and to give expression to the deeper human emotions. The magic of words has played an incalculable part in the long story of human endeavor and human suffering. It may be, therefore, . . . that at this point James is not meaning to disparage the tongue but to draw attention to the magnitude of its achievements" (74, 75). Yet in light of the two illustrations that follow, it is doubtful that James has positive thoughts about the tongue. At best, his thoughts are neutral; but at worst (and most likely), they are negative. The powerful, evil effects of the tongue is what he has in mind in this passage.

Fire's Spark

The third in James's series of metaphors presents the tongue as a fire (vss. 5b, 6). Jewish wisdom literature is filled with sayings that liken the tongue to a flame or a fire. Solomon, for example, proclaims, "The scoundrel plots evil, and his speech is like a scorching fire" (Prov. 16:27; compare 26:21; Ps. 39:1-3; 120:2-4; Isa. 30:27; Sir. 28:22). James may have borrowed this imagery from these ancient sages or even from more contemporary Greco-Roman writers and popular sayings. But the illustration is from everyday Palestine. Ralph Martin has alerted us to the fact that James's setting was a hillside covered with dry brush and wood. "Such an environment is literally a tinderbox just waiting to explode at the slightest spark. The readers of the letter would have no trouble understanding this imagery and appreciating the risk of such a spark's leading to a rapidly spreading fire that would destroy everything in it path" (113). This is the nature of the tongue.

In 3:6 James explicitly addresses the tongue's great potential for destruction. Even though the general meaning of the verse is clear, it is difficult and complex when its detailed parts are examined. Some have found verse 6 to be the most difficult passage in the epistle; others have suggested that the Greek text is corrupt (in the sense of being affected in its transmission); while some go so far as to say the words were added much later by a scribe. Despite its problems, the verse's overall point cannot be misunderstood.

The first point James makes is that the tongue is "a world of evil among the parts of the body" (vs. 6). The word *world* is problematic, thus some commentators have translated the Greek word *kosmos* as "adornment," the sense being that the tongue makes evil attractive. But James does not give this sense to the term when he uses it elsewhere in the epistle. As we noted in our discussion of 1:27, "world" for James is the whole scheme of things, values, and actions that separate us from God and that is at odds with what God requires. The tongue, then, represents the whole scheme of things that are evil. It is possible that Jesus had in mind the evil use of the tongue when he said to the crowd in the presence of the Pharisees and teachers of the law, " 'What goes into a man's mouth does not make him "unclean," but what comes out of his mouth, that is what makes him "unclean" ' " (Matt. 15:11). Then He said to His disciples, " 'But the things that come out of the mouth come from the heart, and these make a man "unclean." For out of the heart comes evil thoughts, murder, adultery, sexual immorality, theft, false testimony, slander' " (Matt. 15:18, 19).

Because the tongue is a world of evil, James's next point is that "it corrupts the whole person" (3:6). The word translated "corrupt" has the sense of staining and polluting. The evil effects of the tongue are those of staining and polluting the individual. The tongue accomplishes the reverse of the pure and faultless religion in 1:27—a religion in which a person is kept from "being polluted by the world." The tongue's effect is the corruption of the whole person. Peter Davids says it creatively: "The flame of the tongue catches the passion: A temper rises; a lust is inflamed. Soon the words, whether an internal dialogue unheard outside or actual speech, burst forth into action. The emotions, the whole of the body, are uncontrollably involved" (*James*, 83).

Not only is the individual body affected by the evil tongue but it "sets the whole course of his life on fire" (3:6). The phrase "course of life" is also problematic. Numerous long essays in commentaries have been written in attempts to explain it. It is a technical term that comes from the "cycle of life" found in the literature of ancient mystery religions in relation to the philosophy of reincarnation. But James does not seem to be using it here in this technical sense. He is making the point that the pollution caused by the tongue is not a temporary and individual phenomenon; it affects all life and all relationships. It exercises its sinister influence throughout the entire course of the person's existence. Many decades ago Lehman Strauss commented homiletically on this text noting that "words spoken carelessly, unwisely, destructively, can set ablaze the whole sphere of our existence, affecting seriously our family life, church life, and community life. . . . Behind every word that is unclean, untrue, angry, divisive, unkind, is Satan himself. I know of one family that has been divided and whose members have not spoken to one another for almost twenty years, all the result of a few unkind words" (132).

Strauss's point, that behind this evil tongue is Satan himself, is in line with James's final point in verse 6. There James says the tongue itself is set on fire by hell. In other words, the tongue receives its power from hell. The term translated "hell" is not *Hades*, the one used most often for hell in the New Testament. James uses *gehenna*, a transliteration of the Hebrew phrase "Valley of Hinnon." This valley was a ravine on the south side of Jerusalem and was the garbage dumb for the city. Because of its constant burning and smoking, it became a symbol of the place of the final punishment of the wicked and the abode of all evildoers and Satan. With this final phrase, then, James is contending that the power behind

the tongue is the devil himself and that with such power, incalculable damage can be brought about. *The Message* paraphrase interprets this verse graphically: "By our speech we can ruin the world,
turn harmony to chaos, throw mud on a reputation, send the whole
world up in smoke and go up in smoke with it, smoke right from the
pit of hell" (vs. 6).

Animals Tamed

James uses as his next illustration the world of dumb animals and
humanity's ability to tame and control them. The psalmist wrote
centuries earlier: "You made him ruler over the works of your hands;
you put everything under his feet: all flocks and herds, and the beasts
of the field, the birds of the air, and the fish of the sea, all that swim
the paths of the seas" (Ps. 8:6-8). James is chagrined at the fact that
we can tame all these kinds of animals (even reptiles and creatures of
the sea!), but "no man can tame the tongue" (3:7, 8).

R. A. Martin has suggested that James is indulging in hyperbole
when he states that the tongue is beyond human control, "for all do
at times control their tongues. It should not be pressed any more
than the hyperbolic claim that every kind of animal had been tamed
(vs. 7). This exaggerated way of speaking serves to impress indelibly
on the reader's mind the great and terrible potential for evil of which
human speech is capable" (38). Martin is not the first person to have
problems with James's super pessimism. Centuries ago, the Pelagians
turned James's statement into a question: "Can any human being
tame the tongue?" To this St. Augustine responded that James does
not say "no one," he said "no human being." "We declare," said
Augustine, "that by the mercy of God, with the help of God, by the
grace of God it can be mastered" (cited in Kugelman, 39). James,
however, did not include those optimistic words; he simply and explicitly asserted that no one is able to tame the tongue. Like all ancient writers of proverbs, James bases his assertion on the realities of
his situation.

James has come to this conclusion because he finds the tongue to
be "a restless evil, full of deadly poison" (vs. 8). Unlike the birds,

reptiles, and creatures of the sea, the tongue is never at rest enough to be brought under control. "In the present context," says Ralph Martin, James presents a "picture of a caged animal pacing back and forth and seeking an opportunity to escape. But whereas it is possible to secure an animal so as to prevent such an escape, this is not so with the tongue" (117).

In saying that the tongue is "full of deadly poison" (vs. 8), James is specifically comparing the tongue to a venomous serpent. Here he is using an Old Testament metaphor as found in Psalm 140:3: "They make their tongues as sharp as a serpent's; and the poison of vipers is on their lips." With this imagery (which incidentally goes back to the Fall of humanity in Genesis 3), James is quite unapologetically explicit in his negative assertions about the tongue and what it accomplishes. For him, the tongue is evil; it is poisonous.

Praising and Cursing

Instead of metaphors, James next uses specific examples to demonstrate how the tongue is full of instability. He says, "With the tongue we praise our Lord and Father, and with it we curse men, who have been made in God's likeness" (3:9). D. Edmond Hiebert says the tongue is "a veritable Dr. Jekyll and Mr. Hyde" (227). It is like John Bunyan's "Talkative" who was "a saint abroad and a devil at home" (Moo, 128). This picture of the instability and duplicity of the tongue was also common in the Old Testament and other Jewish literature. The psalmist writes, "With their mouths they bless, but in their hearts they curse" (Ps. 62:4); and Jesus ben Sirach later wrote, "If you blow on a spark, it will glow; if you spit on it it will be put out; yet both come out of your mouth" (Sir. 28:12, NRSV). James decries this duplicity.

James, of course, is not decrying the tongue's ability to bless. Blessing God was an integral part of daily Jewish life. "Whenever the name of God was mentioned, a Jew must respond: 'Blessed be he!' Three times a day the devout Jew had to repeat the *Shemoneh Esreh*, the famous eighteen prayers called *Eulogies*, every one of which begins, 'Blessed be thou, O God' " (Barclay, 89, 90). But the same mouth that produces this highest, noblest, and purest form of speech, also brings forth cursing.

The Scriptures seem to give mixed reviews to the idea of cursing. Ralph Martin's discussion on this is helpful: "The words of the curse (Deut. 30:19), is another common theme in the OT (Gen 9:25; 49:7; Judg. 5:23; 9:20; Prov. 11:26; 24:24; 26:2; Eccl. 7:21; Sir. 4:5), though there is a certain critical attitude taken to cursing. The NT writers speak out against cursing (Luke 6:28; Rom. 12:14), but Paul sometimes comes close to cursing others (1 Cor. 5:5; Rom. 3:8; Gal. 5:12). There is evidence . . . that formal cursing (that is, the aiming of anathemas at those to be excluded from the church) was not strictly forbidden in the early communities (1 Cor. 16:22; cf. Acts 5:1-11; 8:20; Rev. 22:18, 19)" (119). For James, however, there is nothing positive about cursing. Unlike blessing, it is the lowest, most ignoble, and most impure form of speech. He would agree with Jesus and Paul that we should bless those who curse us, rather than cursing them (see Luke 6:28; Rom 12:14).

James is especially chagrined at the tongue's ability to curse, because these curses are heaped upon creatures made in God's likeness. Here, possibly, the Creation story (particularly Genesis 1:27) possibly lies behind James's words. It is despicable to curse the being that God made in His image. In a sense, our author is saying that when you curse the one made in the *imago Dei*, you are actually insulting and cursing God Himself! It takes an evil and bitter mouth indeed to do that.

Although it would seem that we can be duplicitous by cursing and blessing coming from the same mouth, James seems to make it clear that any mouth that attempts such is in reality only a cursing mouth. He illustrates this by asking two questions that according to the Greek grammatical structure demand a negative answer: "Can both fresh water and salt water flow from the same spring? My brothers, can a fig tree bear olives, or a grapevine bear figs?" (3:11, 12). Or as *The Message* puts it, "Apple trees don't bear strawberries, do they? Raspberry bushes don't bear apples, do they? You're not going to dip into a polluted mud hole and get a cup of clear, cool water, are you?" The tongue can produce only one kind of fruit or one kind of water. Any attempt to mix the good with the bad produces only bad.

■ Applying the Word

James 3:1-12

1. If you are a teacher (in church or society), can you think of an occasion long ago or in recent memory when your words, instead of educating, caused hurt and confusion? How did you deal with the situation? If you haven't dealt with it, how can you use the admonition of James as a "jump-start" to resolve the situation? Jot down your thoughts.
2. Are there instances in the past week when I have opened my mouth and after what came out was spoken, I wished I had held my tongue? How can I control "putting my foot in my mouth"?
3. Do I find myself being angry when I find others in society despising and blaspheming God by their words and actions yet think nothing of it when I curse or speak ill of those I dislike. List occasions when this has been true.
4. If you find yourself to be a person who is zealous for God, yet have an intense hatred for someone or a group of people (whether they be ethnically or religiously different), write a paragraph in your notebook as to what you think James would say to you.

■ Researching the Word

1. Using a concordance, look up the New Testament texts containing the words *teacher, teaching, rabbi,* and *master.* Make a list of the positive and negative characteristics deduced from those passages.
2. In 3:6, James speaks about fires of hell. Look up the word *hell* in a concordance that distinguishes the different origi-

nal Greek and Hebrew words for hell. For this exercise you will need an exhaustive or comprehensive concordance that has Greek and Hebrew helps, such as Strong's, Young's, or Goodrich and Kohlenberger. Based on the biblical texts, what are the differences in each concept? Now look up the word in a Bible encyclopedia or dictionary. Jot down any additional insights found from that investigation.

■ Further Study of the Word

1. See J. Jeremias, *Jerusalem in the Time of Jesus*, 233-245 for illustrations of the high respect accorded to the teacher (or scribe) in first-century Jewish society.
2. A worthwhile compilation of E. G. White's messages to and regarding teachers is found in *Counsels to Parents and Teachers*; see especially 64-71 and 229-271, where the focus is on the teacher.

CHAPTER SEVEN

False and True Wisdom

James 3:13-18

James seems to switch a discussion regarding the misuse of the tongue (3:1-12) to an analysis of wisdom (vss. 13-18). In reality, however, both sections are united. In the first place, the two types of wisdom James analyzes in verses 13-18 are both competing for the use of the tongue—the misuse of which (vss. 1-12) is a sign that false wisdom (vss. 14-16) has had the upper hand.

In second place, both sections are set in the context of contentiousness, disputes, and dissensions. James 3:1-12 demonstrates that the tongue is at the root of all this evil. Verses 13-17 show that the lack of peace and solidarity in the community is due to the fact that false wisdom reigns supreme. The converse is therefore true; when there is true and pure wisdom, there will be peace and unity.

In order to make his point clearly, James does three things. First, he identifies the wise person as one who acts correctly (vs. 13)—not one who only claims to do the right thing but one who actually does it. Second, he describes the marks, nature, and results of false wisdom (vss. 14-16). The vices he lists here are of the world, unspiritual, and originate with the devil himself. Third, he sets forth seven characteristics of true wisdom (vss. 17, 18). These virtues are characteristics of true piety and are heavenly in origin.

■ Getting Into the Word

James 3:13-18

Read through James verses 13-18 carefully twice, then do the following exercises.

1. List both the negative and positive characteristics of wisdom found in this passage. Now browse through Proverbs (especially chapters 1 and 8) and list in your notebook the characteristics of wisdom found there. Compare and contrast the two lists you have made. Write a summary paragraph defining wisdom based on these two lists.
2. Make two columns in your notebook. At the top of one, place the word *vices*, and at the top of the other, put *virtues*. List in the respective columns the vices and virtues found in James 3:13-18, as well as those found in Galatians 5:19-26 and Ephesians 5:1-20. What other vices and virtues (that are not on your list) can you think of that seem to be evident in your worshiping congregation? List them.
3. Compare Jesus' and Paul's teaching on peace in Matthew 5 and Romans 13, respectively, with James's teaching on the same issue. Jot down the similarities. Do these apply equally to the individual, to the church congregation as a body, and even to society at large? Explain why or why not.

■ Exploring the Word

The Wise Person Identified

James is concerned in this passage (3:13-18) to lay out the characteristics of false and true wisdom. But before explicitly and systematically doing so, he gives an opening topic sentence to the paragraph in which he identifies the truly wise person.

The opening phrase "who is wise and understanding among you?" does not give us a clue as to who is the wise person. It seems possible that James, at least in part, has the teachers of verse 1 in mind. The word *sophos* (wise) might be a technical term for the teacher. In Judaism, the teacher, scribe, or rabbi was practically identified with the wise person. He was the one who was recognized as having the highest knowledge and practical wisdom. He was the expert—the one with understanding. James, then, might be using overlapping categories (teachers and wise one) to identify the same individual. Yet, it is possible and seems more than likely that his address has wider application. No doubt he has the wider community in mind and intends to include all his readers.

The person who is wise is challenged to show his or her wisdom by a proper lifestyle and good deeds (vs. 13). This exhortation reminds us of James's challenge in 2:18, where he told his imaginary opponent he will show his faith by what he does. In the same way, he says here in essence: "If you are wise, demonstrate your wisdom by your deeds and your life." In a similar vein Jesus said, "Wisdom is proved right by her actions" (Matt. 11:19). What James and Jesus are emphasizing is that religion and/or wisdom are not cerebral and credal. The focus and emphasis should not be upon what one claims, believes, or thinks. What is more important is what one does. Orthopraxis (right living) is the truer sign of the wise person than orthodoxy (right belief). This is not to discount orthodoxy. But if the lifestyle does not match the belief, the latter is to be discounted. James will not back off from this stance. He consistently reiterates his position that "actions speak louder than words" (1:22-27; 2:12, 13; 2:14-26).

The truly wise and understanding person will not only demonstrate his or her wisdom by a good life and appropriate deeds but such actions will be characterized by humility and meekness (3:13). In putting forth this position, James was bucking the norms of his Greco-Roman world. Meekness and humility were not universally sought-after virtues. People who were seen to be meek were associated with the servile, ignoble, and debase. Leon Morris notes that "it was held that a real man would stand up for his rights and not allow himself to be trampled on. It was humiliating not to be accorded one's full rights and one's proper place. Rivals must not be allowed to usurp one's proper privileges and the like" (86).

The Scriptures, on the contrary, consistently present meekness and humility as hallmarks of the child of God. Moses is presented as the epitome of humility: "Now Moses was a very humble man, more humble than anyone else on the face of the earth" (Num. 12:3). Over and over, Jesus reiterated the importance of meekness. "Blessed are the meek," He says, "for they will inherit the earth" (Matt. 5:5). He exhorts His hearers to come to Him if they are burdened, and He will give them rest. "Take my yoke," He continues, and "learn from me, for I am *gentle and humble* in heart" (11:28, 29; compare 23:8-11). This same emphasis on meekness and humility, especially in situations of potential conflict, is found throughout the writings of Paul and other New Testament writers (2 Cor. 10:1; Gal. 6:1; Eph. 4:2; 2 Tim. 2:25; Titus 3:2; 1 Pet. 3:15). Likewise, here James identifies the wise and understanding person in his community as the one whose life and behavior is characterized by meekness and humility.

False Wisdom Identified

In verses 14-16 James presents the opposite characteristics of the wise person identified in 3:13. In doing so he identifies false wisdom, which he will later contrast with true wisdom.

Sophie Laws has alerted us to the obvious comparison between James and "the opening chapters of 1 Corinthians, where Paul both attacks the contentiousness associated with the Corinthian 'parties' (1:10-13; 3:3 f.), and also seeks to provide a proper interpretation of Christian 'wisdom' (1:18–2:15; 3:18-21)" (160). Although the situation in Corinth and that of James's community seem to be radically different, the fact remains that similar vices were at the heart of the dissension and divisive spirits. But these vices were not limited to Corinth and James's community. The Pauline epistles are filled with lists of vices that were common to most of the churches. And Paul seemed to have a kind of "fixed" sequence in his ethical instruction catalogues (Dibelius, 210). For example, in Galatians 5:20 we find "hatred, discord, jealousy, fits of rage, selfish ambition, dissensions, factions." And in 2 Corinthians 12:20, Paul speaks about "quarreling, jealousy, outbursts of anger, factions, slander, gossip, arrogance, and disorder." James's list of vices is not as extensive, but the three or so that he highlights certainly encompass all of Paul's.

The first vice James mentions is *zēlos* (3:14; "bitter envy" in the NIV). The word itself is neutral and can be basically translated zealous or jealous. Positively, "it could mean the noble emulation which a man felt when confronted with some picture of greatness and goodness" (Barclay, 91). It is this type of "zeal" that Phineas was commended for when he defended God's honor and drove a spear through an Israelite and the Midianite woman (Num. 25:11-13). Or, in the case of Jesus, His zeal led Him to whip the animals out of the temple, while overturning tables and chasing out the sellers of doves (John 2:17).

James's use of the word *zēlos* is not positive, however. The truth is that there is a fine line between positive zeal and negative jealousy. Peter Davids points out that "zeal can easily become blind fanaticism, bitter strife, or a disguised form of rivalry and thus jealousy; the person sees himself as zealous for the truth, but God and others see the bitterness, rigidity, and personal pride which are far from the truth" (*Commentary*, 151). This is exactly what Paul condemns in many of his lists of vices (Rom. 13:13; 2 Cor. 12:20; Gal. 5:20) and what James speaks of here.

The second vice is *eritheia* ("selfish ambition"). The word has an interesting evolution. William Barclay notes that it "originally meant *spinning for hire* and was used of serving women. Then it came to mean any work done for pay. Then it came to mean the kind of work done solely for what could be got out of it. Then it entered politics and came to mean that selfish ambition which was out for self and for nothing else and was ready to use any means to gain its ends" (91). Thus it appears in Aristotle where it means "a self-seeking pursuit of political office by unfair means" (Davids, *Commentary*, 151). In James, as in other New Testament writings (for example, Rom. 2:8; Gal. 5:20; 2 Cor. 12:20), the meaning of the term is not limited to the political realm. The emphasis here is on "the inclination to use unworthy and divisive means for promoting one's own views or interests" (Ropes, 246).

James instructs those persons who harbor such bitter envy and selfish ambition not to boast about "it" (3:14). The "it" most likely refers to "wisdom" in verse 13. James is telling them to stop (the Greek construction with the particle *mē* and the imperative indicates that they should stop something they are presently doing): "Stop boasting; stop being arrogant about your wisdom; stop denying or lying against the truth, you who are full of bitter zeal and selfish divisive ambition!"

This false wisdom about which they are boasting is the opposite of the wisdom that James will characterize in verse 17. True wisdom is a gift from God Himself; false wisdom has no divine origin. James characterizes it with an advancing series of adjectives that express its evil nature: earthly, unspiritual, demonic (vs. 15).

The first term, "earthly," has a neutral significance in Greek, as is clear in Jesus' words: "I have spoken to you of earthly things" (John 3:12). But for the most part, it is used in the New Testament epistles in a derogatory sense with negative connotations. It refers to what is inferior, imperfect, transitory, weak, and evil (1 Cor. 15:40; 2 Cor. 5:1; Phil. 3:19). James's usage is clearly intended to give it a derogatory and evil sense. The false wisdom has nothing heavenly in its origin. Its essence is earthly.

The second term, *psuchikos* ("unspiritual"), always has a negative meaning in the New Testament. In most contexts, it is contrasted with *pneuma* ("spirit"). It is important to note that in much of ancient Greek philosophy, the human person was divided into three parts: body, soul, and spirit. Barclay defines each thus: "The body (*sōma*) is our physical flesh and blood; the soul (*psuchē*) is the physical life which we share with the beasts; the spirit (*pneuma*) is that which man alone possesses, which differentiates him from the beasts, which makes him a rational creature and akin to God" (93). The writers of the New Testament, being Jewish (and thus holistic in their anthropology), did not thus divide up the individual ontologically. However, they used the terms to characterize people's relationship (or nonrelationship) to God and His Spirit. Jude, for example, describes the false teachers as *psuchikoi*—"who follow mere natural instincts and do not have the Spirit" (Jude 19). But it is Paul who uses the term more extensively. Interestingly, it is when he is speaking about wisdom (like James) that he employs the adjective the most. Sophie Laws summarizes Paul's usage well:

> Paul, dealing in Corinth with claims to a special spiritual understanding, describes this variously as a wisdom "of this world" (1 Cor. 1:20), "according to the flesh" (1:26), "of men" (2:5), "of this age" (2:6), and as put forward "in words which human wisdom teaches" (2:13); epithets which would add up to a comprehensive definition of what is meant by being *psuchikos*. . . . Against that Paul describes his own preaching as of Christ "The wisdom of God" (1:23 f), taught by the Spirit, and received by the *pneumatikos* but not the *psuchikos* man (2:13-15) (Laws, 162).

> Decades later gnosticism (a Christian heretical philosophy which had its roots from the time of Paul) taught that the "unspiritual" persons are the ones "who do not partake of special knowledge and enlightenment [and] remain at the level of the *psuchē*; that is, the merely human man living as part of the 'natural' world order, sharing the life-force of the animals, responsive only to his senses and untouched by the divine spirit" (Laws, 161, 162).

Possibly James is using the term "unspiritual" with similar connotations. This false kind of wisdom not only has its origin in the earth but it is animal-like; "it is the kind of wisdom which makes an animal snap and snarl with no other thought than that of prey or personal 'survival' " (Barclay, 93). Whether this is exactly what James had in mind or not, it is clear that the unspiritual wisdom is devoid of God's spirit.

But it is more than that; it is demonic (3:15). This third adjective is meant to shut the door to any questions as to the origin of false wisdom. It is inspired by the devil. The readers who harbor bitter envy and selfish ambition, and who think their wisdom is inspired by God, only fool themselves. James lets them know without qualification that their wisdom has its genesis in the world of demons.

James has one more thing to say about those who possess this false wisdom and who have this bitter zeal and selfish ambition. In verse 16 he describes the effect of their actions: "There you find disorder and every evil practice." James's concern is for communal unity and peace, but these persons are bringing instability to the community. The word he uses here for disorder or instability (*akatastasia*) is the noun form of the adjectives he uses in 1:8 and 3:8 to describe the "double-minded person" and the "double-speaking" tongue. The first is unstable in all his or her ways; the second is a restless evil. Douglas Moo notes that this word "is used in Luke's Gospel to describe the 'tumults,' the uprisings, and revolutions, that will typify the period preceding the *parousia* [second coming] (Luke 21:9). And Paul, pleading with the Corinthians to refrain from an unbridled, unorganized display of individual spiritual gifts in the assembly, reminds them that 'God is not a God of confusion but of peace' (1 Cor. 14:33)" (134). As a matter of fact, this passage in James reminds us not just of this situation with tongues but of all the other situations (from dissensions to immorality) in the Corinthian church that destroyed the unity and peace of that community (see the entire first epistle to the Corinthians).

As far as James is concerned, all wisdom that leads to disunity and evil practices is false. And the possessors of this false wisdom among his readers are clearly identified: they are the ones who have envy and selfish ambition; they are at the root of the disorder; they are the cause of much suffering in the community.

True Wisdom Identified

James leaves the best for the last. After outlining the negative nature of false wisdom that exists in a jealous and selfish atmosphere, he now presents the positive characteristics of true wisdom. This true wisdom is not earthly, unspiritual, and demonic as the former; it is heavenly (3:17). Like the good and perfect gifts James spoke of earlier (1:17), this true wisdom is from above. Here again he follows the Old Testament wisdom traditions and the Jewish sages in their emphasis that God is the source of all wisdom. For example, the famous passage in Proverbs comes to mind, in which wisdom is portrayed as a feminine being, alongside God at Creation (Prov. 8:1-31). Much later, Jesus son of Sirach began his book of wisdom sayings with the poetic bicolon, "All wisdom is from the Lord, and with him it remains forever" (Sir. 1:1, NRSV). Toward the middle of the book, Sirach also has wisdom praising herself saying, "I came forth from the mouth of the Most High, and covered the earth like a mist" (Sir. 24:3, NRSV). About seven decades before James wrote his words, these ideas were expressed by a learned Jewish sage from Alexandria: "For she [wisdom] is a breath of the power of God, and a pure emanation of the glory of the Almighty" (Wisdom of Solomon 7:25, NRSV).

James does not dwell on the origin of wisdom. His interest is in what it is, or more accurately, what it should produce, for as Moo points out, most of the seven adjectives he uses "describe what wisdom does rather than what it is" (135). In a sense, wisdom in James functions as does the Spirit in Galatians 5:22, 23. Granted, there is a little verbal resemblance between the two passages, yet the essence of the "fruit of the Spirit" in Galatians is the same as the characteristics of wisdom in James. The same is true of "love" in 1 Corinthians 13. Wisdom, the Spirit, and love all produce heavenly behavior.

Of the seven characteristics of wisdom listed by James, the first and overarching one is purity. It is doubtful that James is thinking in this context of sexual or moral purity. Rather, it is more likely he is thinking of how Psalms and Proverbs used the word. In Psalm 12:6, we read that "The words of the Lord are flawless"; that is, pure, genuine, without deceit, and without ambiguity. And in the Greek translation of the Old Testament (the version that James most likely used), the sage speaks of the ways of the righteous as pure, in contrast to the ways of the crooked person (Prov. 21:8)! "This purity, then means," suggests Peter Davids, "that the person partakes of a characteristic of God; he follows God's moral directives with unmixed motives" (*Commentary*, 154). This purity is exactly the opposite of the selfish ambition in verse 14, for it lacks the crookedness that comes with jealousy and selfishness.

Also incompatible with jealousy and selfish ambition is the second characteristic of true wisdom: peace loving. James will speak more about this in verse 18. But at this point he wishes to highlight this attribute as a major one in his sevenfold list. In this context he wishes it to be clear that true wisdom produces not only a right relationship between God and humans but between persons and persons. True wisdom will not allow a person to hurt by his tongue or by any other means.

The third characteristic in the series is "considerate." The idea behind the Greek word *epiekēs* is that the person who has this attribute is gentle, noncombative, does not get defensive or angry under provocation. In a sense, this characteristic goes hand in hand with the next, *eupeithēs* (submissive). The emphasis here is that the person is open to reason—quite the opposite of the person who is combative and defensive. This person is "easily persuaded." This is not to say that the individual is gullible, weak, without convictions, and easily swayed by every wind (compare 1:5-8). But he or she is willing to give deference to others, to listen carefully (instead of using the tongue unwisely), and submit instead of attacking.

An attribute that is close to James's heart is that of "mercy." He says here that wisdom is "full of mercy and good fruit" (3:17). Earlier in our discussion of 1:27–2:26 we noted that the merciful ones are those who have deep concerns for persons who are suffering economically and that deeds of mercy are the good fruits the merciful will produce. It is interesting to note that most people in the Greco-Roman world define "mercy" as "pity for the person who is suffering unjustly." The New Testament, however, goes beyond that. William Barclay reminds us that "in Christian thought *eleos* means mercy for the man who is in trouble, even if the trouble is his own fault. Christian pity is the reflection of God's pity; and that went out to men, not only when they were suffering unjustly, but when they were suffering through their own fault. We are so apt to say of someone in trouble, 'It is his own fault; he brought it on himself,' and, therefore to feel no responsibility for him" (96, 97). James, like Jesus and other New Testament writers, certainly would give thumbs down to such an attitude. For him, mercy is a virtue that is expended freely even to the unworthy.

The penultimate virtue is impartiality. The idea behind this word could be either that there is freedom from prejudice, or the idea of "not doubting," "unwavering," "having a single outlook," "sincere in opinions." This latter definition seems more likely, since the word appears in the list next to the final characteristic of wisdom: "sincere." In this last characteristic, the emphasis is on a lack of hypocrisy. James attacks the tendency to be hypocritical, or even "clever." This latter idea of cleverness reminds me of the Anancy stories, which are so much a part of my boyhood society. These ancient stories feature a clever spider (Anancy) who would use whatever means possible to confound and defeat his opponent as well as to work all kinds of evil. Anancy was, and still is, a hero in a number of cultures. James condemns Anancyism. He pleads for sincerity.

Even though James has completed listing the seven characteristics of wisdom, he has not quite finished his argument. In verse 18, he singles out for special emphasis the virtue of "peace." It is obvious why he does this. The entire chapter, and much of the next, is concerned with the disunity within the community due to the disputes; bitter, contentious quarrels; fights; arguments; and general disturbances of the peace. For James, the person who possesses true wisdom is a peacemaker. That person will be a pacifist.

The idea of a "pacifist" has not been a popular one in this century of wars, in contradistinction to the first four centuries of Christianity when Christianity and pacifism were synonymous. But James is reminding us that peacemaking (the true meaning of pacifism) is an essential virtue in the lives of God's people. Let us remember with Gordon Poteat that the word *pacifist* "is from Latin roots that are the equivalent of the Greek terms in this sentence, makers of peace. As to the means to be used to achieve peace, there is room for differences of opinion, but can there be any dispute that the vocation of every Christian, whatever his status in society, is to make peace, to strive to secure those conditions and relationships that will make possible goodwill, concord, and cooperation instead of hatred, strife, and conflict?" (51, 52).

■ Applying the Word

James 3:13-18

1. In my home and/or family experiences, do I find myself exhibiting the characteristics of the "earthly wise-person," or by God's grace am I exhibiting the "heavenly wise-person" characteristics? Is there a difference when I am at church and in church circles as to the characteristics I exhibit? Are they different at work and/or at school? If Yes, what can I do to make my life more consistent?

2. Did I find myself becoming angry, combative, and defensive this week? Was it under provocation and out of character, or was it because of a weakness in my character? How did I deal with the situation?

3. Did I find myself in a position where I was a peacemaker this past month? What was the response to my actions or words? Reflect on the pros and cons. If the cons outweighed the pros, would I do it again? Would I change my strategy? Have I written off the other party/parties who rejected my peacemaking efforts?

4. Do I tend to show mercy only to those who find themselves in negative situations that are not due to their own fault? Do I agree with the position that the New Testament challenges us to show mercy even to those whose troubles are brought about by their own errors of judgment or behavior? If No, explain. If Yes, make a list of persons (that fall in the latter category) to whom you will attempt to show mercy within the next month.

■ Researching the Word

1. Look up the word *wisdom* in a Bible dictionary or Bible encyclopedia. Can you find characteristics of wisdom in those articles that were not in the list you made in the "Getting Into the Word" section of this chapter? If so, list the additional characteristics.

2. Look up in a Bible dictionary each of the words used by James to characterize true and false wisdom. Jot down explanations of each of these that were not given in the "Exploring the Word" section of this chapter.

■ Further Study of the Word

1. For E. G. White comments on peacemaking and mercifulness, see *Thoughts From the Mount of Blessing*, 21-24; 27, 28; 69-75.
2. For an excellent discussion on the philosophy of peacemaking, followed by stories illustrating his point, see J. Yoder's little book *What Would You Do?*
3. For further insights on the heavenly true wisdom versus the earthly wrong kind of wisdom, see W. Barclay, *The Letters of James and Peter*, 91-98; and S. Laws, *The Epistle of James*, 158-166.

PART FOUR

James 4:1–5:6

Tensions

CHAPTER EIGHT

Moral Tensions

James 4:1-12

After much negative exhortation in chapter 3, James ended the third part of his epistle on a positive note: "Peacemakers who sow in peace raise a harvest of righteousness" (vs. 18). But this positive note would not last long. The situation was anything but peaceful. The tensions (religious, political, economic, etc.) had peaked and were at the root of disintegrating relationships. These violent tensions had to be addressed more extensively than had been done previously.

At the outset James sets forth the reasons for the quarrels, fights, and conflicts in the community (4:1-3). In doing so he presents the theological grounding of the tensions. The problem is that instead of God being chosen as friend, He is the enemy, and the world and the devil are companions (vss. 4-6). But James calls for repentance, asking his hearers to submit themselves to God, knowing that He will exalt them (vss. 7-10). James, however, does not end on this soft positive note. He has one more negative moral concern before he addresses economic tensions. The slandering and the judging must stop if the turbulent relations are to be reversed (vss. 11, 12). In this passage, James will not soft-pedal the issues. The serious situation demands language of intensity.

■ Getting Into the Word

James 4:1-12

Before reading this passage, pray that the Lord will help you to be honest with the text and will help you not only understand it in its context but to make application of it to your life and to the wider society. After that, read the passage two or three times and then respond to the following questions.

1. What types of quarrels and fights do you think James is speaking of in verses 1, 2? Are they literal or metaphorical? Explain.
2. In verse 1 James says that conflicts come from the desires that battle "within" you. Is the word "within" referring to that internal something within the individual, or is it speaking of the evil desires within the community or group? Explain.
3. Explain the phrase "friendship with the world" (vs. 4). What did James mean then? How would you interpret it for your situation today?
4. Explain your deepest feelings as you read the series of commands in verses 7-10. Do you find James coming across harsh and exacting? Or do you feel quite comfortable with his language? Explain.
5. Explain the term *law* (vss. 11, 12). Is it used differently here than James uses it elsewhere in the epistle? With the help of a concordance or by scanning the text, find those other passages and compare and contrast them with these verses.

■ Exploring the Word

Fights and Quarrels

The two nouns found in the first sentence (4:1) establish the acute, chronic tension and hostility that existed in James's community. These fights and quarrels were not petty conflicts. They were major causes of social dislocation and death. This is shocking to acknowledge, and many biblical interpreters are wary of admitting the literal nature of the author's concern. But Bo Reicke is certainly correct when he advises us: "We have no right to explain away or tone down the author's statement about these troubles; as though he exaggerated or did not mean to be taken seriously (as some expositors do out of respect for the early church, or for other reasons). Historical honesty demands that we acknowledge the situation as it was, rather than re-create it as we or others should like it to have been" (45).

If we intend to read the text rigorously, we must first ask: What is James speaking about when he uses these two nouns: *polemoi* ("fights," "wars") and *machai* ("quarrels," "fights")? These words are most often used to describe physical, literal conflicts between nations, communities, and/or individuals. Yet there are those who interpret the words metaphorically or soften them to refer to hatred among a body of believers or merely to verbal battles among James's audience. We cannot rule out the possibility that James is referring to such verbal conflicts. After all, the overwhelming point of the previous chapter is that the tongue is a violent and destructive instrument (see especially 3:3-6).

A mere metaphorical interpretation for "fights" and "quarrels" or "wars" and "fights" seems to be inadequate, however. Ralph P. Martin points out that for one to limit James's concerns in this way, he or she would have to overlook "the fact that the letter of James was most likely written in a period when murder was accepted as a 'religious' way to solve disagreement" (146). A classic example is Saul's murderous threats against the primitive Christian communities and individuals (Acts 9:1; John 16:2). Martin has convincingly argued that the strong language of the text, especially 4:2, indicates that James has much more in mind than metaphorical niceties (144). James is addressing the literal wars, fights, murders, and quarrels of his time and society.

In order to put these verses in historical perspective, we should remember that James is possibly writing prior to the A.D. 66 war with Rome. The years leading up to the war saw the intensification of the Zealot revolution. The Zealots were a highly nationalistic party within Judaism that was determined to dethrone Roman rule in Palestine by whatever means necessary.

We must note here with Michael Townsend that the Zealots were not one monolithic party, but the word *zealot* "must be regarded as something of an umbrella term covering a number of national interests" (212). It is interesting to note that Simon the Zealot was a disciple of Jesus—Luke 6:15. Yet despite differences among those calling themselves zealots, there was a basic commitment to over-throwing Rome's stranglehold on Palestine through bloodshed. Thus they waged a guerilla warfare in which terrorism of a "hit and run" variety was widespread.

The attacks and hatred of the Zealots were leveled not only against the Roman imperial forces. They opposed all who collaborated with Rome and strove to preserve the status quo. Particularly offensive to them were the Sadducean hierarchy and the priestly party who supported Roman rule and the laissez faire approach that allowed the local authorities to rule in whatever manner they wished. But also offensive to the Zealots were the wealthy who became rich from the Roman economic policies—or lack of policies that would benefit the poor. It is in this context that James writes. His community was a Zealot-infested society. And "No doubt," says Martin, "different positions on the most viable attitude toward Roman rule prompted heated discussion and possible physical confrontation" (146).

It seems to me that it is precisely this major problem of physical wars and fights that James is addressing in these verses. We miss a major concern of the author if we limit the interpretation of the text to small, petty infighting and quarrels in the church. Thus, I agree with Leon Morris in his observation that what James says "has relevance to a wider circle than quarrelsome Christians. To an age as eager for peace and as much given to war as ours, these words about the root causes of wars come home with force and relevance. For the fact is that if we promote a warlike spirit it is only to be expected that we will have wars, and this whether on the grand scale between nations or on the small scale between church members" (86). The sad fact is that we are so quick to apply even this interpretation of the verse to "the other side." For example, in the 1980s it would have been easy for us in the West to apply these words to the South African black freedom fighters or the Communist guerrillas in Latin America. We would argue vehemently that James condemns their fights, killings, and civil wars. Yet at the same time, we would have no qualms in supporting the Nicaraguan freedom fighters/contra rebels or European anti-Communist fighters! If James were writing in the last decades of the twentieth century, I believe that his message would be pointed to both sides of the fence—to all the modern Zealots.

Although James is very concerned about physical tensions and conflicts, he possibly is even more concerned about their source. He, therefore, tells his readers that conflicts "come from your desires that battle within you" (4:1). Literally, the Greek phrase for "within you" is "in your members." The term *members* has been translated "bodies" in various parts of the New Testament (compare Rom. 6:13; 7:23) with reference to the individual. In many of these texts, the focus is on the place within the person where the passions reside. If James is using members thus, his thoughts would most likely parallel his discussion in 1:13-15 regarding the *yetser*. In our treatment of that passage we noted that in much of Jewish thought the seat of evil passion was located in the *yetser*. If this is what James has in mind here, his argument would be that fights and quarrels arise from desires within the individual *yetser*.

In this context, however, it seems doubtful that James is harking back to the earlier discussion in verses 13-15. Rather than an individualistic concern, his concern is communal. The fighting and quarreling arise because of the desires that battle within the community over not only religious issues but over other societal and political issues. It seems more than likely that there were warring factions among his readers—on the one hand, those who wanted peace and the use of peaceful means to accomplish these goals and on the other hand, those who saw violence as the only means possible. Passions and desires ran high.

The word translated "desire" (4:1) is *hēdonōn*, from which we get our English words *hedonist* and *hedonism*. Although we tend to think of this concept in purely sexual and sensual tones, the word itself simply means "pleasure" or the more neutral term "desire." However, in many instances the word carries more weight than mere pleasure or even sensual lust. In Titus its juxtaposition with a list of vices similar to those James is concerned with indicates the negative weight of the word. There we read, "At one time we were too foolish, disobedient, deceived, and enslaved by all kinds of passion and pleasures [*hēdonais*]. We lived in malice and envy, being hated and hating one another" (Titus 3:3, 4; cf. Luke 8:14; 2 Pet. 2:13). With this in mind, a more appropriate translation and interpretation of the term would be "passion"—passion for war, passions for gain, etc. It was this intense negative passion within the community that was the root cause of the fights, quarrels, and tensions among James's readers.

It is worthwhile noting that many ancient writers also suggested that the root of many of the problems and evils in the world was desire. William Barclay cites a few: "Lucian writes, 'All the evils which come upon man—revolutions and wars, stratagems and slaughters— spring from desire. All these things have as their fountainhead the desire for more.' Plato writes, 'The sole cause of wars and revolutions and battles is nothing other than the body and its desires.' Cicero writes, 'It is insatiable desires which overturn not only individual men, but whole families, and which even bring down the state. From desires there spring hatred, schisms, discords, seditions and wars' " (99). In a similar way, James identifies the source of the fights and quarrels.

How intense was this passion and desire? James tells us in 4:2. "You want something but don't get it. You kill and covet, but you cannot have what you want. You quarrel and fight." Over the centuries it has been difficult for many commentators to accept that James was actually accusing his readers of killing (see Wells, 96; Kugelman, 46). Many have followed the Renaissance scholar Erasmus and replaced "kill" with "jealous," thus making the text read, "You are jealous and you covet." Such interpreters find it preposterous for James to accuse his readers (who are thought to be exclusively Christians) of killing. This position is surprising, for even within our historical moment we find that in international conflicts (for example, World War II) Christians fight against Christians. And in civil conflicts the same is true. The 1994 Rwandan civil war clearly demonstrates this when thousand of Rwandans were slain by fellow members in their own local churches!

It is also unfortunate that other interpreters argue that James is not talking about a present situation; rather, he is predicting the future. We argue on the contrary, that James is saying that the tensions in the community involve actual killing. But they also involve "envy."

In this phrase, the word used for "envy" is *zēloō*, from which we get our words *zealous* and *jealous*. However, it is possible to translate it "envy" or covet." If this is the correct interpretation of the word, the New Revised Standard Version's punctuation of the verse is helpful: "You want something and do not have it; so you commit murder. And you covet something and cannot obtain it; so you engage in disputes and conflicts." This is supported by a number of biblical illustrations. The story of Ahab and Naboth's vineyard is a classic example of the power of envy and covetousness that resulted in murder (1 Kings 21:1-29; compare the narrative of Cain and Abel in Gen. 4:2-16).

James, however, may have the literal meaning of the word *zēloō* in mind. In this case he would be not only telling his readers that they kill but that they are fanatic zealots. Bo Reicke suggests that the sentence be interpreted as follows: "You drive people to death by being zealots" (45). The reference then would be to the violent activities of the Zealots. The text would then be punctuated like the NIV but with a different interpretation for the word translated "envy": "You want something but you don't get it. You kill and you are fanatic zealots, but you cannot have what you want. You quarrel and fight" (4:2). In this case, James is not only condemning their violence but also telling them that it is useless. Social violence has not, and will not, accomplish what they passionately desire.

James presents an alternate way. Instead of killing, murder, mayhem, and zealotry as a method to accomplish their goals, why not ask God? He is, in fact, reiterating Paul's instructions to the Philippians: "Do not be anxious about anything, but in everything by prayer and petition, with thanksgiving, present your requests to God" (Phil. 4:6). James is telling his readers that peace will not come by means of the sword. Peace and whatever other desires they have will come only by petitioning God.

The readers of the epistle, however, will respond to James saying, "We did try prayer first. We did ask God; but we did not receive. God helps those who help themselves. So we are trying the sword."

But James responds: "When you ask, you do not receive, because you ask with wrong motives, that you may spend what you get on your pleasures [hēdonais]" (4:3). Their prayers fail because they were not prepared to give up their hostile ways and become peacemakers (3:18). They wanted God to answer on their terms. James says No. God gives on His terms. His terms are those of peace, unity, and humility.

Friends of the World and Enemies of God

The second paragraph of this chapter contains further stinging rebukes. James, instead of addressing his readers as killers and murderers, addresses them as adulterers (4:4). If it is true that James literally means killers in the previous verses, then it seems logical that he is speaking of literal adultery here. Thus, the King James Version adds to the word *adulterer*, *adulteress* even though the latter is not found in the original Greek.

However, there is nothing in the context of James's epistle that suggests that literal adultery was a major problem in his community. If this be the case, we must presume that the word is being used metaphorically in the sense in which the Old Testament prophets used it when Israel broke her covenant relationship with God. This relationship was often portrayed in marital terms, as in the case of the word of the Lord Jeremiah. God told him to proclaim to Jerusalem: "I remember the devotion of your youth, how as a bride you loved me" (Jer. 2:2; compare Isa. 54:1-6). But Israel was constantly unfaithful, broke the covenant, and apostatized. This was stigmatized by the prophets as adultery. The most classic example was the experience of the prophet Hosea, whose marriage to an adulterous woman was a symbol of God's relationship with His people (Hos. 1-3; 9:1; see also Isa. 54:1-6; 57:3; Jer. 3:6-10, 20; 13:27; Ezek. 16:23-34). The marriage imagery passed into Christian usage for the relationship of Christ and the church, in which Christ is the bridegroom and the church is the bride, and both are faithful to each other (2 Cor. 11:2; Eph. 5:23-32; Rev. 19:7; 21:9). James is, therefore, using the adultery image in this metaphorical manner. In similar fashion,

Jesus employed the language of the prophets and called His contemporaries "a wicked and adulterous generation" (Matt. 12:39; compare 16:4; Mark 8:38).

James's focus might not be merely the idea of infidelity, as in the case of prophetic writings such as Hosea, Isaiah, and Jeremiah. His emphasis most likely is on the style of the sinner. In this case, the pertinent Old Testament passage would be Proverbs 30:20: "This is the way of an adulteress: She eats and wipes her mouth and says, 'I've done nothing wrong.' " The style of the adulteress, says John Schmitt, is that "she commits her deed and feels no remorse. She is detached from any consequence of her evil ways. This sinner has lost, or is suppressing, the moral sensitivity that should characterize a friend of God" (336).

James gives a wake-up call to his hearers by letting them know that this adulterous relationship (which he calls "friendship with the world"—4:4) is at enmity with God. To be a friend of the world is to be a hater of God. There is no compromise. No numbing of the sensibilities will change that. It is clear-cut, either/or: You either love the world or you love God (1 John 2:15, 16). In a similar vein, Jesus lectured His hearers on the Mount of Beatitudes: "No one can serve two masters. Either he will hate one and love the other, or he will be devoted to the one and despise the other. You cannot serve both God and Money" (Matt. 6:24).

Again we must emphasize that James is not suggesting that we withdraw or become obnoxiously separate from the world or society in general. "World" for James is the whole scheme of things, values, and actions that separate us from God and that is at odds with what God requires. Such things and values may be found within the community of believers, as well as outside the community within the wider society. Thus in James's theology, if one is in a friendly relationship with such a value system, that person in reality is an enemy of God.

But he says more in a very difficult verse: "Or do you think Scripture says without reason that the spirit he caused to live in us envies intensely" (4:5)? This verse is difficult for a couple of reasons. In the first place, James cites it as Scripture. But no such verse occurs in the Old Testament—at least no recognizable verse. Possibly this could either be a quote from a lost book or a summary of an Old Testament passage. Or James could be expressing in proverbial form an idea from many Old Testament passages. The problem is, unless we understand the idea he is attempting to communicate, it will be difficult to trace the scriptural source.

This leads us to the second, and main, reason for the difficulty in understanding the verse. At the heart of the problem is the word *spirit*. In the Greek sentence, it can be either the subject or object of the sentence. And to complicate matters, it can be either the Holy Spirit or the human spirit. Both the footnotes or margins in the NIV as well as the accepted text illustrate the perplexity. You will note that the first alternative in the NIV has God as the subject: "God jealously longs for the spirit that he made to live in us." This is the translation the New Revised Standard Version accepts. In it, God is the subject who is jealous of His adulterous people. The other alternative has "spirit" as the subject: "The Spirit he caused to live in us longs jealously." The problem with this translation is that this would be the only place in James in which the Holy Spirit is mentioned (if Holy Spirit is what is meant). The NIV text instead takes the spirit as the subject but interprets it as the human spirit. Yet it is not clear what James would mean by "The human spirit yearning intensely." Ralph Martin suggests a fourth alternative: "The Spirit of God made to dwell in us opposes envy" (149).

It seems to me that the best choices we have are either the first or last alternatives. The first because it ties the verse into the discussion of the previous verse, affirming God as a jealous God, demanding total, unreserved, unwavering allegiance to Him alone. The last alternative makes sense if it is tied into the following verse. In this case, James is setting up two sets of parallelism:

A. The Spirit of God made to dwell in us opposes envy.
B. He gives us more grace (4:5, 6a).

A1. God opposes the proud.
B1. But He gives grace to the humble (vs. 6b).

It is difficult to choose between the alternatives. What is certain, however, is that God opposes whatever would come under the rubric of friendship with the world, and that includes envy and pride and all the violence James spoke of earlier.

Although God's demands are strict and this opposition to evil and His jealously are intense, James assures us that His grace is abundant. He says, "but He gives us more grace," that is, His grace is more abundant than His judgment. The recipient, however, is not anyone and everyone. The quotation from Proverbs 3:34 ("God opposes the proud, but gives grace to the humble") demonstrates the limitation of God's gift of grace. Only those who humble themselves and submit to His will can receive this gift (4:6).

Submission and Exaltation

The "then" (vs. 7) with which James begins the next paragraph indicates that the quotation from Proverbs is intimately tied in with the ten imperatives that follow. The fact that all these imperatives are grammatically placed in the Greek aorist tense indicates that James wishes his readers to grasp the urgency of the message (R. P. Martin, 152).

The first attitude James calls for is submission (vs. 7). The person who has given up pride and has humbled himself or herself before God can receive grace only if that one is submissive. Yet, James calls for more. Not only do his readers have to submit to God; they also have to resist the devil.

The New Testament is filled with texts that present the devil as a spiritual power that must be resisted. The most classic example of such a confrontation is between Jesus and Satan in the wilderness prior to our Saviour's ministry (Matt. 4:1-11; Luke 4:1-13). But equally impressive are passages in the letter to the Ephesians in which the church is admonished to put on the whole armor of God and fight against the devil's schemes (Eph. 6:10-18; compare 4:27) or the passage in 1 Peter 5:8, 9, which reads, "Your enemy the devil prowls around like a roaring lion looking for someone to devour. Resist him."

James assures his readers that when they resist the devil he will flee from them. This is an assurance to all who submit themselves to God. This is very much in line with the thoughts of Ellen White when she noted that the weakest person who finds refuge in Christ will cause the devil to tremble and flee (White, *The Desire of Ages*, 131).

The negative emphasis of resisting the devil gives way to the positive call to "come near to God and He will come near to you" (4:8). James, however, desires his hearers to do more than that. He challenges them, as sinners, to wash their hands. The language is derived from ancient Jewish rites in which the priests were required under the penalty of death to wash their hands and feet before entering the sanctuary or temple and performing their duties (Exod. 30:17-21). By the first century A.D., the rabbis had made it a ritual requirement that all Jews wash their hands before eating in order to avoid being ritually unclean. Jesus challenged this when He said to His disciples, "Don't you see that whatever enters the mouth goes into the stomach and then out of the body? But the things that come out of the mouth come from the heart, and these make a man 'unclean.' For out of the heart come evil thoughts, murder, adultery, sexual immorality, theft, false testimony, slander. These are what make a man 'unclean' " (Matt. 15:17-20). Like Jesus, James rejects the ritualistic washing but focuses on the "inward disposition with outward social concern and action" (R. P. Martin, 153).

Just as the Jacobean community is called to "wash their hands," so they are now (or further) admonished to purify their hearts (James 4:8). (This reminds us of the psalmist's call for clean hands and pure hearts—Ps. 24:3, 4). In the first place, James's emphasis is on their deeds and actions; in the second place, it is on their thoughts. In this latter instance, he addresses them as "doubleminded." This is the same word he used in 1:6-8, in which their "two-soulness" was characterized by doubting and instability. In this context, the issue is one of allegiance. Ralph Martin's insights are helpful here:

> The chief problem before James' audience is their hesitancy and indecision, as they wavered in their allegiance to God

and were tempted to be drawn away to false hopes and into "diabolic" paths led by Zealot factionalists. . . . In effect . . . it is the choice between God and his enemy, whether called the devil (4:7; cf. 3:15: "demonic" is the source of this "wisdom") or Beliar (as in T. Asher 3:2) or the world (4:4). These forces stand implacably opposed to God whose tender desires for his people's integrity are nonetheless set against all forms of "envy" (4:5; also, 3:14-16) and "strife" (3:14), which is so debased that it entails "waging war" and "murder" to achieve its patriotic and superficially attractive—but really perverted—ends (143).

James is adamant that such double allegiance is impossible. Such thoughts and behavior need purifying.

James is not satisfied with the Old Testament priestly language of cleansing and purifying (4:8). He now uses prophetic language. Like the major and minor prophets of the Old Testament, he gives a ringing call to repentance. He cries out, "Grieve, mourn and wail. Change your laughter to mourning and your joy to gloom" (vs. 9).

Of course, we must not read these words as if they were intended to "kill joy." They are not an invitation to asceticism. The fact is, though, that in this context the only appropriate response that should accompany repentance is sorrow, especially since the emotion that characterizes their enmity to God is foolish laughter and senseless rejoicing.

The humility that is reflected in the grieving, mourning, and wailing, will result in exaltation. "Humble yourselves before the Lord," says James, "and he will lift you up" (vs. 10). This teaching of James mirrors his position in 1:9-11 in which the humble poor are exalted and the proud rich are debased. It also repeats, in imperative form, Jesus' statement at the end of the parable of the Pharisee and the tax collector: "He who humbles himself will be exalted" (Luke 18:14). And in Paul's epistle to the Philippians, Christ is set forth as the classic and supreme example of the submission-exaltation motif: "He humbled himself and became obedient to death—even the death on the cross! Therefore God exalted him to the highest place" (Phil. 2:8, 9).

Slandering and Judging

Up to this point, James has attacked a series of serious moral evils that are at the root of much of the tensions in his community. But he has one more to address before he turns to economic tensions. This moral issue is one that is closely tied to his earlier concern with the tongue and its misuse (see 1:26; 3:1-12). His specific concern at this point is slander. He says, "Brothers, do not slander one another" (4:11). The Greek negative particle, *mē*, with the present imperative grammatical structure, indicates that his readers were habitually speaking against and maligning each other. James admonishes them to desist such defamatory behavior.

The Bible is filled with condemnation of the practice of slandering, irresponsible and malicious gossip, and simply speaking evil against one another (Lev. 19:16; Ps. 50:20; 101:5; Prov. 18:8; 26:22; Rom. 1:30; 2 Cor. 12:20; 1 Pet. 2:1). Yet, as William Barclay notes, "There are few activities in which the average person finds more delight than this; to tell and to listen to the slanderous story—especially about some distinguished person—is for most people a fascinating activity" (111).

James gives an interesting reason why slander is so outrageous: "Anyone who speaks against his brother and judges him speaks against the law and judges it" (4:11). Such behavior not only affects the victim but it is an attack on God's law. We are not certain which law James is referring to here. But it seems likely the reference is to the royal law of Leviticus 19:18 ("love your neighbor as yourself"), especially since this verse comes soon after the command, "Do not go about spreading slander among your people" (vs. 16). A person who loves his or her neighbor will be faithful to the law and will not judge or slander him or her.

James gives one other reason for his condemnation of slander and judging. It is usurpation of the prerogative of God: "There is only one Lawgiver and Judge . . . but you—who are you to judge your neighbor?" (4:12). James did not, but he could have effectively added the words of Jesus, "Do not judge, or you too will be judged" (Matt. 7:1). The person who slanders his or her neighbor has, in effect, passed judgment upon him or her. By infringing upon the prerogative of God, such a person will be judged severely by the one and only true Lawgiver and Judge!

■ Applying the Word

James 4:1-12

1. When did my worst quarrel and/or fight take place? Was it worth it? Would I handle the situation differently today? If Yes, how?
2. When was the last time I engaged in a religious or theological quarrel and/or fight? Was it worth it? What were the gains? What were the losses?
3. Am I a pacifist? If Yes, why? If No, why not? Are there times when Christians should go to war? If Yes, when? Would it make a difference if I were fighting against a fellow Christian or a non-Christian? Explain.
4. How do I react when I don't get what I want (or even *need*) from God? What is my normal rationalization? Explain.
5. How can I be friends with people in the world without being friends with the world?
6. Do the imperatives in verses 7-10 remind me of a pastor or leader who seems to be always preaching judgment, "calling sin by its right name," and calling his or her congregation to repentance, always emphasizing the dos and the don'ts? Do you think of these dos and don'ts positively or negatively? How do you feel about them after reading James?
7. Are there long-lasting feuds in my life or in the life of my local church because of slander, malicious criticism, or malignment of character? Is there anything I can do to resolve these feuds? List two or three suggestions.

■ Researching the Word

1. In your concordance, look up the words *lust* and *desire*, particularly those translated from the Greek word *epithumia* (you will need to use the language helps available in an exhaustive or comprehensive concordance). List the times it is used positively, negatively, or neutrally. Based on the contexts, what times would you translate the word differently in some cases? Which ones?
2. Look up in your concordance significant words (*submit, wash, wail*) that occur in verses 7-10 and note similar texts in the Old and New Testament. Choose three or four of those texts and briefly summarize their contexts. How do they compare and contrast with James's exhortation?

■ Further Study of the Word

1. For extensive treatments of the argument for a Zealot context in this passage, see M. J. Townsend, "James 4:1-4: A Warning Against Zealotry?" and R. P. Martin, *James*, 137-157.
2. For treatment on questions relating to resisting the devil, see E. G. White's chapter "The Victory" in *The Desire of Ages*, 124-131.

CHAPTER NINE

Economic Tensions

James 4:13–5:6

In this section, James continues to address his concerns regarding the tensions within his community. But instead of issues such as fighting, quarreling, slandering, etc., he returns to a topic that is very close to his heart—the issue of poverty and wealth. Here he summarizes and strengthens what he said previously. As he addresses the economic question, his purpose, as always, is to give comfort to the suffering community and at the same time to spell out the final judgment on the rich.

Three groups of wealthy persons are singled out for special mention in James's epistle. In 2:6, 7 they are the financiers and bankers. Here in 4:13-17 they are the merchants, and in 5:1-6 they are rich agriculturalists. We must be aware, however, that these classes are not distinct. The activities are different functions of the same individual or group of individuals. But in this final outburst, James attacks the rich from the perspective of two different spheres of their existence. As they operate within these spheres, they bring suffering upon the poor. It is for this reason that James attacks and opposes them.

In the first part of his remarks (4:13-17), he zeroes in on the financiers who desire to carry on business as usual without concern for anyone—neither God nor the poor. Then in the second section (5:1-6), he lambasts the rich agriculturalist and big landlords because of their luxurious living. It is only after he has laid low the economically powerful that James can admonish the economically marginal to be patient (vs. 7).

■ Getting Into the Word

James 4:13-17

Read 4:13–5:6 through once to get a feel for the unity of the passage. Then read 4:13-17 again carefully before responding to the following questions and exercises.

1. Read the parable of the talents in Matthew 25:14-30. In what ways is that parable similar to this passage in James? In what ways do they differ? Why does one seem negative and the other seem positive? Explain.
2. Read the parable of the rich fool in Luke 12:16-21. Jot down the parallels you find between that parable and James's message in 4:13-17.
3. Read Jesus' words in the Sermon on the Mount regarding worrying over material things (Matt. 6:25-34). Make a list of ways in which these words of Jesus relate not only to James's concern but also to the two parables in the above question.

■ Exploring the Word

Business as Usual

James 4:13 commences the author's last attack on the rich. The manner in which he addresses them indicates that he has no intention of being friendly. The first two words, *age nun* (translated "now listen" in the NIV) are not meant to be a friendly phrase. Both here and in 5:1 where it is repeated, it is the signal for an attack in the denunciatory style of the Old Testament prophets. Biblical interpreters who suggest a milder translation (than the brusque one intended by James) see the addressees as ambitious, industrious small-business people of the first century, who with courage are planning their future operations as traveling traders. It is suggested that James is not objecting to their desire for profit or their planning but to the fact that they have not put God first in their plans and deliberations.

A careful reading of the text and its context, however, seems to make it certain that James's speech is based on the socioeconomic realities of his situation and milieu. His attack is leveled at those involved in the big commercial enterprises of merchants, commercial schemers, and business persons. They are arrogant types. The way James skillfully spells out their activities and their plans demonstrates this view—we will go . . . and stay . . . and carry on business . . . and make money—as does his mention of a period of a year. These were business schemers who went where they wanted, stayed as long as they wanted, and did what they wanted. They were not little shopkeepers in Jerusalem, Antioch, or any of the small towns in Palestine. These were big, rich traders.

In order to better understand James's attack, it is worthwhile to understand travel in the first century for such purposes as indicated in this verse. In my 1981 dissertation "Poor and Rich in the Epistle of James" (193-218), I discussed this at length. I noted that this period was the halcyon days for a traveler, particularly those who were engaged in business enterprises. The Roman peace (*Pax Romana*) had transformed the world around the Mediterranean, making it easy and safe for traveling and enterprise. Commerce increased as mines, quarries, smelters, and food-processing facilities were built. This, of course, not only facilitated and enhanced trade and commerce; it also increased the level and extent of economic exploitation. Greedy and arrogant merchants could easily go from city to city, port to port, where the latest activity had blossomed, and gather greater wealth unto themselves at the expense of the generally poor populace.

Joachim Jeremias in his book *Jerusalem in the Time of Jesus* has alerted us to the fact that Jerusalem and Palestine were as much a part of international commercial activities as major cities in the Mediterranean basin. Owners of capital had always been attracted to Jerusalem. Such capitalists included Jews of the Diaspora who had grown rich, tax collectors, wholesalers, and others. Merchants had much respect for Jerusalem as an attractive market for commerce. Even the high priest, as well as the lesser priests, was engaged in extensive commercial activities (*Jerusalem*, 27-31, 49, 71). Accumulation of wealth was the goal, and these business people would do whatever was necessary to reach that end.

Sociohistorical description of the first-century Greco-Roman world, and particularly Palestine, has shown the ready availability of raw material and the ease with which astute entrepreneurs could reach their destination and dispose of their goods. This information makes more understandable James's repetition of these confident merchants' words: "Today or tomorrow we will go to this or that city, spend a year there, carry on business and make money" (4:13).

James condemns such presumptuous confidence when he responds to their arrogance by categorically stating: "Why, you do not even know what will happen tomorrow. What is your life? You are a mist that appears for a little while and then vanishes" (vs. 14). James's language, though stronger, parallels that of the ancient sage who said, "Do not boast about tomorrow, for you do not know what a day may bring forth" (Prov. 27:1).

Even more striking is the parallel with Jesus' parable of the rich fool recorded in Luke 12:16-21. This most satirical of Jesus' parables is a classic example of the arrogant, presumptuous, commercial enterprises and activity during the time of Jesus and James. For this rich fool to say "I will tear down my barns and build bigger ones, and there store all my grain and my goods. And I'll say to myself, 'You have plenty of good things laid up for many years. Take life easy; eat, drink, and be merry' " (Luke 12:18, 19), without concern for anyone but himself, was arrogance at its height. In a slightly similar fashion Jesus ben Sirach speaks of the one who "becomes rich through diligence and self-denial, and the reward allotted to him is this: when he says, 'I have found rest and now I shall feast on my goods!' He does not know how long it will be until he leaves them to others and dies" (Sir. 11:18, 19, NRSV). Also in another intertestamental writing, woes are pronounced upon those who "acquire silver and gold in unrighteousness . . . [their] riches shall not abide . . . [but shall] speedily ascend from them" (1 Enoch 97:8-10; cited in Maynard-Reid, "Poor and Rich," 219).

It seems to me that James, like the speakers and authors of the above passages, does not see the traders of his day as honest business persons. But James's language is stronger. His *age nun*, "now listen," is as intense as in 5:1. It is more than likely that for him these merchants, like just about all first-century Palestinian merchants (see my extensive description of this situation in "Poor and Rich"), are unscrupulous, unrighteous, arrogant, and oppressive. That is why they are accused of boasting in their arrogance, their cleverness, luck, and skill. But all such skillful, arrogant, cleverness is of no use. As James said in 1:10, 11, those who fall into that category are like the flower that fades away under the scorching heat. Here he says, they are like a mist that vanishes.

Life's Like a Mist

The Greek term for "mist" (*atmis*) can be translated "vapor" or "smoke." But in this context, in which the focus of the attack includes sea merchants, the idea of mist is most relevant. The Mediterranean mist that rolls in from the sea and quickly disappears is a perfect metaphor for the transient, insubstantial nature of those merchants who thought they had it all and knew it all.

James is possibly not only drawing on the actual geographical phenomenon of his setting but may also have Old Testament usage in mind. For example, in Hosea the image of mist is used in the context of judgment, as it is in James. In poetic language, Hosea relates God's anger against Israel. He writes: "Therefore, they will be like the morning mist, like the early dew that disappears, like chaff swirling from a threshing floor, like smoke escaping through a window" (Hos. 13:3). In their arrogant certainty, these presumptuous commercial schemers forgot that life is frail—that they are only mortal and human creatures. They failed to recognize that their life was in the hands of God and so was their continuing existence and plans.

Instead, James suggests that all commercial and economic activity must include the premise, "If it is the Lord's will" (4:15). It is worthwhile to note that this expression is essentially non-Jewish and was popular among Greeks, Romans, and Arabs. It was, however, adopted by Jews and was even considered mandatory by some Jewish rabbis before an enterprise was undertaken. Today the expression "God willing" is used popularly and glibly, devoid of its deep religious content. James is not exhorting a flippant use of the expression. He is calling for a recognition of who is really in charge.

Rather than making that ultimate recognition, these rich business people "boast and brag"—literally, they boast in their arrogance (vs. 16). The word *boast* (*kauchaomai*) is many times used positively in the New Testament. One of the results of justification, according to Paul, is that we "boast" in the hope of God's glory (Rom. 5:2). But here in James the object of boasting is not the hope of God's glory but arrogance (*alazoneia*). This latter word has an interesting root. It refers to the wandering quack (a parallel of the "medicine-man" of early American and other non-Western societies). As Paul Cedar notes, "This quack offered cures which were not cures; he boasted of things which he was unable to do" (89). James's merchants, however, were convinced they knew what they were doing and were certain of their goal. Yet, in reality, they were "wandering in an unreal world of speculation and boasting to others about what they think they have found there" (Tasker, 104). James says, "All such boasting is evil" (4:16).

Sin of Omission

As James comes to the end of this first of two concurrent diatribes against the rich, he throws in a maxim which does not seem to fit well with the rest of the passage. He writes: "Anyone, then, who knows the good he ought to do and doesn't do it, sins" (vs. 17). The "then" indicates that James intends this to be a concluding statement for these verses. When placed in the context of the merchants, it is possible that James is pointing out that these business schemers know better and fail to do accordingly. Thus their actions are sinful.

Too often we have relegated the sin of omission to a minor place in our hierarchy of errors. Thus a person who neglects to do something has merely missed an opportunity for obedience. For James, he or she has sinned. This is true especially when it has to do with the social realities of the poor. In James, the failure to do is significant, as the indictment in 2:14-26 clearly indicated. Faith without words is dead. Having faith, but omitting to house and feed the poor, still places one in the category of sinner.

Douglas Moo has alerted us to the fact that the Scriptures make it abundantly clear that "sins of *omission* are as real and serious as sins of *commission*. The servant in Jesus' parable who fails to use the money he was entrusted with (Luke 19:11-27); the 'goats' who failed to care for the outcasts of society (Matt. 25:31-46)—they are condemned for what they failed to do. Another teaching of Jesus reminds us very forcibly of James's words here: 'That servant who knew his master's will, but did not make ready or act according to his will, shall receive a severe beating' (Luke 12:47)" (158). In this context, James adds to the examples of Jesus: These merchants and commercial schemers arrogantly carry on their business without a consciousness of God's will; and, it can be inferred from the rest of James's book, not only neglect to take care of the poor but are their oppressors through their scheming. Such business persons are not just acting foolish or mildly bad; James categorically says they sin.

■ Getting Into the Word

James 5:1-6

Read 5:1-6 two or three times. Meditate for a moment on the passage. Pray. Ask God for wisdom to grasp, understand and accept His word as it reads; then do the following exercises:

1. Read Matthew 6:19-34 and Luke 6:20-36. Make a list of the sayings of Jesus in these passages that are similar to the sayings of James in this passage. Do you find any differences? What are they?
2. Compare and contrast Jesus' parable of Lazarus and the rich man (Luke 16:19-31) with this passage. Why is there such a focus on luxury?

3. **Read Revelation 18:9-24. Make a list that compares and contrasts Revelation's woes with James's diatribe against the rich.**
4. **There seems to be no call to repentance in these verses in James. Explain why he fails to call the rich to repent of the sins he chastises them for in this passage.**

■ Exploring the Word

The Woe

In 4:13-17 James denounced a spirit of arrogant financial scheming. Now he addresses a spirit even more wicked and obnoxious. It is one that is selfish, tyrannical, and oppressive. The actions are so oppressive and exploitative that the cries of the sufferers "have reached the ears of the Lord Almighty" (5:4).

As in 4:1, the opening words of the address, *age nun* (translated "now listen" in the NIV), is intense; it is insistent and brusque. Its repetition here raises James's denunciation to an even higher level. This is demonstrated in the harsh language of the passage. His message to the rich is not a friendly one. The Authorized Version's translation of the opening, therefore, may be much closer to James's intent and feeling than the more modern translations. There we find the classic words, "Go to, now you rich men" (5:1).

James sees the rich as an ungodly social class. This seems evident from the fact that he used the Greek vocative case in his grammatical construction. He is not focusing on an individual; he is highlighting a class. It is also evident that they are ungodly; because in 4:13-17 James is incensed that they leave God out of their planning. So they are an ungodly social class—as a *class*. This is probably why there are no words of repentance for them. There is no hope for any rich person as long as they belong to that class. Our author promises only judgment and damnation.

In this sharp invective against the rich, James tells them to "weep" and "wail" or "howl" (5:1). This latter word (*ololuzō*) is onomatopoeic—a word that carries its meaning in its very sound. William Barclay tells us that it means more than simply to "wail." It means to "*shriek.*" "It depicts the frantic terror of those on whom the judgment of God has come" (115).

The words *weep* and *wail* echo the imperatives of doom found in the writings of the Old Testament prophets and is more often than not tied in with the Day of Judgment—The "Day of the Lord," the "Day of Yahweh." For example, in the oracle against Babylon, Isaiah writes: "Wail, for the day of the Lord is near; it will come like destruction from the Almighty" (Isa. 13:6; see also his oracle against Moab in 15:3; compare Zech. 11:2).

The rhetorical language of the passage in James not only parallels the style of the Old Testament prophets and previous apocalyptic writings but echoes the teachings of Jesus. The classic example is recorded by Luke in Jesus' sermon on the "level place" (6:17). In this sermon (unlike Matthew's Sermon on the Mount), Jesus not only has beatitudes but he speaks woes, the first of which is "woe to you who are rich, for you have already received your comfort" (vs. 24).

Decades after James's and Jesus' woes on the rich, the apocalyptic writings of Revelation utilize similar woes to highlight the economic aspect of its message. The Revelator has the kings of the earth and the merchants who share in the luxury of Babylon weeping and mourning over her and crying saying, "Woe! Woe, O great city, O Babylon, city of power! In one hour your doom has come!" (Rev. 18:10; compare vss. 9-24).

We must note that the language of the prophets, the apocalyptic writers, Jesus, and James were for the most part, not intended to influence the rich. In many instances they were not even part of the writer's audience. Thus James's remarks were not given to the rich as a call to repentance. They were aimed at the suffering poor. They were intended to be words of comfort and consolation to those undergoing trials due to oppression by the rich. These poor persons were assured that ultimate judgment would certainly be meted out upon those who oppressed them.

The Crime of Luxurious Living

James sees the rich as committing two crimes: (1) luxurious living and (2) oppression. The first is dealt with in 5:2, 3, and 5. The second is discussed in verses 4 and 6. The verses that address the issue of luxurious living speak of expensive articles that have been hoarded and note that all these signs of wealth are worthless. Those riches will one day become evidence against the rich and will be part of the judgment on them.

In many places in the Scriptures, such luxurious living is denounced. The prophet Amos was famous for his eloquent denunciation. With great emphasis he cried out, "Woe to you who are complacent in Zion. . . . You lie on beds inlaid with ivory and lounge on your couches. You dine on choice lambs and fattened calves. . . . You drink wine by the bowlful and use the finest lotions" (Amos 6:1-7).

Luke, more than any other author in the New Testament, highlights Jesus' concern with the evils of a luxurious lifestyle. The parable of the rich man and Lazarus (Luke 16:19-31) is a case in point. The fact that the parable begins with a description of the rich man (Dives)—he was "dressed in purple and fine linen and lived in luxury every day" (Luke 16:19)—signifies that this lifestyle is a major point in the story. That Dives could live such a life of dissipation while Lazarus wallowed in his sores and begged is testimony to the fact that Christ had a problem with that type of lifestyle. This was especially true since the rich man refused to share with Lazarus.

Although the Matthean words of Jesus could be at the back of James's mind ("Do not store up for yourselves treasures on earth where moth and rust destroy and where thieves break in and steal"—Matt. 6:19), James might also be thinking of Jesus' words as recorded by Luke, "Sell your possessions and give to the poor. Provide purses for yourselves that will not wear out, a treasure in heaven that will not be exhausted, where no thief comes near and no moth destroys" (Luke 12:33).

Even if the Matthean and Lukan sayings were at the back of James's mind, at the forefront was the actual situation around him. The wealthy of the first-century possessed much clothing, and hoarding clothing was popular. For example, one Lucullus claimed to have 5,000 cloaks at home (Maynard-Reid, "Poor and Rich," 225)! The typical wealthy person would heap up not only clothing but carpets and all manner of furniture in their homes. For James, all these signs of wealth are worthless.

In his denunciation, James tells the rich: "Your wealth has rotted, and moths have eaten your clothes. Your gold and silver are corroded" (5:2, 3). It is significant that James uses the perfect tense here—the Greek tense, which normally signifies something that has happened in the past with continuing results. However, it seems more than likely that James is using what is known as "prophetic perfects." The prophet sees the events in his "vision" as already realized. The judgment is so certain that it can be described as already present. James thus portrays with certainty the imminent final condemnation of the rich.

This judgment he spells out even more graphically in verse 5: "You have lived on earth in luxury and self-indulgence. You have fattened yourselves in the day of slaughter." Alex Motyer notes that "the picture is fearfully vivid. They are like so many unthinking beasts, luxuriating in their rich pasture day after day, growing fat by the hour and careless of the fact that each day, each hour, brings the butcher and the abattoir nearer. Only the thin beast is safe in that day; the well-fed has made itself ready for the knife" (168).

The Crime of Oppression

Following his attack on the luxurious living of the first-century rich, James now takes up the cause of the poor agricultural workers who are being oppressed and exploited (vs. 4). Both in ancient times and in the modern era, agricultural workers—sharecroppers, migrant workers, field hands, etc.—have been among the most exploited of people. At the heart of James's concern is the failure to pay the worker an honest wage. Biblical commentator, Lehman Strauss's reaction in the 1950s to James is insightful: "Without engaging myself in the long unsettled dispute between capital and labor, I will merely say that no labor leader ever spoke out more severely and sternly against the unfair practices of some employers who pay laborers less than a living wage in order that they might add more to their vast possessions. . . . Such a practice is labeled 'fraud' by God" (187).

This fraud has initiated the cry of the laborers against the perpetrators of the fraud! The cry brings to mind the cry of the blood of Abel (Gen. 4:10) and the cry against Sodom and Gomorrah (Gen. 18:20, 21). The rich landowners in James are guilty of a crime that, like the blood of Abel, cries out for vengeance from the ground where it was shed. In similar fashion, the cry parallels that brought against Sodom and Gomorrah. In this case, the Lord said, "The outcry against Sodom and Gomorrah is so great and their sin so grievous that I will go down and see if what they have done is as bad as the outcry that has reached me" (Gen. 18:20, 21).

Like the sins of Sodom and Gomorrah ("Now this was the sin of your sister Sodom: She and her daughter were arrogant, overfed and unconcerned; they did not help the poor and needy," Ezek. 16:49), the crimes of the rich landowners seem to be the ultimate for James. They are so grievous that the cries of the poor, who are treated so fraudulently, have reached the ears of the "Lord Almighty," or the "Lord of Host" (*Sabaoth*). This expression is one of the most majestic titles for God in the Old Testament. As "Lord of Sabaoth" He was the commander of the cosmic hosts—the stars, the angels, His entire dominion (see Ps. 103:20-22). This title emphasizes not only majesty but transcendence. God Almighty is the supreme sovereign, the Creator of all existence. It draws attention to His sovereign omnipotence. This supreme, sovereign, Almighty God hears and will defend His lowliest, and seemingly most insignificant, creatures against the ungodly oppressors.

Lehman Strauss again notes that "God never stands by idly while the poor are being oppressed. Whatever else James has in mind, he certainly is not omitting the fact that God is on the side of those who are wronged. . . . God regards every act of cruelty and oppression. . . . Let every helpless victim of oppressors be comforted. God is not an uninterested bystander" (188). The exploited laborer can also take courage from God's response to the oppression by the taskmasters of Egypt upon the Israelite slaves: "I have indeed seen the misery of my people in Egypt. I have heard them crying out because of their slave drivers, and I am concerned about their suffering. So I have come down to rescue them from the hand of the Egyptians" (Exod. 3:7, 8). In the same way the psalmist used language of a divine answer to prayer when he wrote: "In my distress I called to the Lord; I cried to my God for help. From his temple he heard my voice; my cry came before him, into his ears" (Ps. 18:6).

The specific problem James is addressing here is the failure to pay the workmen who mow the fields of the wealthy landowners. Injunctions against such a failure to pay go as far back as the Mosaic laws. In Deuteronomy 24:14, 15 we find the regulation, "Do not take advantage of a hired man who is poor and needy, whether he is a brother Israelite or an alien living in one of your towns. Pay him his wages each day before sunset, because he is poor and counting on it. Otherwise he may cry to the Lord against you, and you will be guilty of sin" (see Lev. 19:13; Mal. 3:5). These instructions are affirmed in rabbinic literature. For example, in the Babylonian Talmud we read, "Whoever withholds the wages of a hired laborer transgresses these five prohibitions of five denominations and one affirmative precept as follows: Thou shalt not oppress thy neighbor; neither rob him; thou shalt not oppress an hired servant that is poor. The wages of him that is hired shall not abide all night with thee. At his day shalt thou give him his hire; and neither shall the sun go down upon it" (Maynard-Reid, "Poor and Rich," 228). Like James, the intertestamental wisdom writing of Jesus ben Sirach goes even further than the Mosaic precepts and the rabbinic injunctions and states that the refusal to pay an employee is murder. The entire passage is insightful: "The bread of the needy is the life of the poor, whoever deprives them of it is a murderer. To take away a neighbor's living is to commit murder; to deprive an employee of wages is to shed blood" (Sir. 34:25-27, NRSV; see James 5:6).

I have written extensively elsewhere on the situation that James is addressing in these verses. I noted there that the widespread problem of big landowners dominating the economic scene and oppressing the poor was of concern to others in James's time. For example, the Roman writer Seneca, who lived from 4 B.C. to A.D. 65, wrote that the big landowner "adds one estate to another, evicting a neighbor either by buying him out or by wronging him" (Maynard-Reid, "Poor and Rich," 229).

The dominance of the big landlord over the marketplace was assured in a number of ways. In the first instance, he had far better produce to sell than his poor competitor, who was usually his tenant. To these tenants he would rent the inferior segment of the property, thus ensuring his produce was qualitatively better. And even the payment he received from the tenant had to be their best products, thus leaving them with the worst material to sell in the marketplace. I noted in my doctoral dissertation that "The small farmer had to eke out a living from a small plot of land that was generally in the stony and unproductive hill country, while the wealthy landowners controlled the fertile lowlands. Ben Sira recognized the sorry situation when he said of such a poor farmer: 'on the height of mountains is his vineyard and the earth of his vineyard is washed down into the vineyards of others' " (Maynard-Reid, "Poor and Rich, 241, 242).

With situations such as the above, the small, poor farmer, of necessity, was driven to give up his farm and become a day-laborer for the wealthy landowner. And in many instances, this debt-ridden laborer was forced to sell himself and his family into slavery. These are the laborers, the workmen, who James says mow the field of the rich. He is clearly sympathetic to their plight because of the oppression brought upon them by their employers.

In his anger James accuses these rich persons of murder when he writes: "You have condemned and murdered innocent men" (vs. 6). There are those who will say that murder in this verse is not intended literally; rather, it is a metaphor for the economic oppression by the rich on the poor. But it seems clear that James has in mind not simply economic tyranny but physical violence as well. The mechanics of economic oppression causes the death of the poor. When persons are deprived of their living and are left without the basic essentials of life, death follows. That is murder (see 1 Kings 21; Luke 16:19-31).

After accusing the oppressors of murder, James makes one final point. The NIV translates the phrase as "who were not opposing you" (vs. 6). In other words, the murderous landlords were killing their laborers, and the latter died passively without putting up a resistance. The Greek allows the possibility of a different translation, however. Instead of the subject of the verse being the suffering laborers, the subject should be God. Looked at in this way, the phrase should be translated as a question: "Should He not oppose you?" If it is recognized this is the closing line of an *inclusio* that began in 4:6, then we hear James's point clearly: (1) God opposes the proud; (2) you behave arrogantly; (3) should he not oppose you? (4:6–5:6). This line of argument fits well into the denunciatory nature of James's final diatribe against the rich. The focus is not on the passivity of the suffering poor but on God's social-action justice on their behalf.

■ Applying the Word

James 4:13–5:6

1. As I evaluate my life, do I find myself obsessed with one or more of the following: *time* ("today or tomorrow;" "for a year"); *purpose* ("we will go"); *place* ("to this or that city"); *goals* ("to carry on business"); and *reward* ("make money")? What can I do to put these into perspective and not make them an obsession in our fast-moving society?
2. Do I find myself using the expression "God willing" flippantly, or do I stop and think through what it means when I use such expressions? Are there times when God expects us (if it is His will) to use common sense instead of taking what could be an "easy way out" by just saying "God willing?" Explain.
3. When I ask myself the question "What is life?" do I usually get a negative response (like the one in James 4:14)? Are there times when it is appropriate to think of life positively? When would be such times?
4. If I were fortunate enough to inherit $1,000,000 today, how

would I use it? Write down general goals and specific ex-
penditures.
5. As an employer (whether of a large multinational corpora-
tion or of a yard keeper, etc.), do I pay my employee the
wage I would wish to receive if I were in his or her shoes? If
James were writing to me today, what would he say about
the last remuneration I paid to someone who performed a
service for me—both in terms of how much, and also, when
it was paid? Write out your thoughts in a private diary.

∎ Researching the Word

1. Using a concordance, look up New Testament usage of the
word *rich*. Write a paragraph or two that gives a summary
explanation of the New Testament's view of the rich person.
Compare your findings with the article on "rich" in a Bible
dictionary. How do your conclusions compare and contrast
with James's description?
2. Look up the words *weep* and *howl* (or *wail*) in a Bible concordance. Identify five or six passages in which the word (or
words) is used in judgment. Jot them down in your notebook with a brief explanation of their context and state what
parallels they have with James.
3. Look up the words *clothes* or *clothing* in a Bible dictionary.
Can you identify times when clothing was the downfall of
certain individuals or groups? Jot them down. Do the same
for *gold* and *silver*.

∎ Further Study of the Word

1. For detailed insight on trade and commerce in Jerusalem in
the first century, see J. Jeremias, *Jerusalem in the Time of
Jesus*, 27-57.
2. For a more detailed exegetical and sociohistorical description
of these passages, see P. Maynard-Reid, *Poverty and Wealthy
in James*, especially chapter 5 ("The Merchant Class and

the Poor") and chapter 6 ("The Rich Agriculturalists and the Poor"), 68-98.

3. See P. J. Hartin's article "Come Now, You Rich, Weep and Wail" for both an exegesis of James 5:1-6, as well as an example of a biblical passage applied to the wider context of a particular modern society—in this case, South Africa.

4. For a biblical study on the call for the rich to share their wealth with the poor, see P. Maynard-Reid, "Called to Share."

PART FIVE

James 5:7-20

Responses
to Suffering

CHAPTER TEN

Patience

James 5:7-12

James's fifth section (5:7-20) parallels in a number of ways the opening section of the epistle (1:1-18). First and foremost, both emphasize trials and sufferings. This highlighting of suffering at the beginning and the end of the book forms a kind of inclusio, a bracketing, for the entire theme of the epistle. At the beginning of his letter, James acknowledges the fact that there is, and will be, trials of many kinds (1:2). Here, in conclusion, he suggests a number of ways his readers should respond to the sufferings brought on by the trials alluded to in his letter.

The first of these responses is a call to patience (5:7-12). The exhortations and warnings in these verses also mirror those found in the opening section. In both instances, patient perseverance is being promoted. The reader can, without fear, exemplify this virtue because God is in control; He will not only give the wisdom to endure (1:5), but His coming will put an end to those who are at the root of the trials and suffering (5:7-9).

■ Getting Into the Word

James 5:7-12

Read verses 7-12 carefully at least twice and then do the following exercises, keeping your James notebook handy for answering the questions and jotting down important insights.

1. Why does James tell his readers to be patient (vs. 7)? What

is the immediate context of his exhortation?

2. James's statement in verse 9 seems to interrupt the flow of thought begun in verse 7. What do you think occasioned this interruption? Do you find anything in the previous verses that might have triggered the introduction of these two sentences? Write down your discovery.

3. Browse through the book of Job. Do you find Job consistently patient and persevering throughout his entire ordeal? If your answer is "No," list three or four occasions when he lost his patience. Then explain James's use of Job as an example in light of your findings.

4. In parallel columns write out Matthew 5:34-37 and James 5:12. Jot down the similarities and differences between both sayings.

5. Explain what you think James means when he says "do not swear" (vs. 12). Does this include taking an oath in court or prior to assuming political office? Why, or why not?

6. Do Jesus and James really mean that Yes and No (Matt. 5:37; James 5:12) must always be the answer under all circumstances? Are there times when it is best not to give a direct answer to a pointed question? List such times and explain.

■ Exploring the Word

Patience and the Lord's Coming

The call for patience in suffering (vs. 7) can be, and has been, read as a general exhortation for all children of God who are undergoing hardship or distress. However, the presence of the Greek word *oun* (then) at the beginning of the verse indicates that this call is tied into the previous paragraph. The imperative "be patient" should not be read separately from verses 1-6. James's concern is still the role of the suffering poor in relation to the oppressive rich. What should be the response of the poor?

In verses 1-6 James outlined the oppressive and exploitative practices of the wealthy class; he condemned their luxurious and extravagant living and then ended by stating that God will oppose them. Since God will take care of the rich, James's readers need not follow the Zealots or the Zealot-like types in their violent campaigns against the ruling Romans and their wealthy local representatives. Instead, James advises them to be patient until the Lord's coming (vs. 7). They should not lose patience and give up to vindictiveness and despair, since James assures them that the day is coming when their oppressors will be judged, and a great reversal will take place (see 1:11; 4:14).

We must raise the question at this point (if we are to be faithful to the text and its context), "What is the event referred to as 'The Lord's coming' (5:7)?" There are two possibilities. The first, and most popular, is that it refers to Jesus and His second coming. The strongest argument for this position is that the word used for "coming" is *parousia*, which is a technical word adopted in the New Testament for the return of Christ at the end of the age. The word was often used in a secular context in association with an official visit of the Roman emperor to a city or province and thus became a fitting word for Jesus' second advent (see 1 Cor. 15:23; 1 Thess. 2:19; 4:15; 5:23; 2 Thess. 2:1; 2 Pet. 1:16; 3:4; 1 John 2:28; Matt. 24:3, 27, 37, 39).

The second interpretation argues that "Lord" here does not refer to Jesus but has reference to God and His day of judgment. In the immediate context of chapter 4 and 5:1-6, it is God who is the Judge (note in vs. 4 the reference to "Lord Almighty"; compare vs. 9); and it would be quite awkward to understand "Lord" in verses 10, 11 as any other person but God, not Christ (Easton, 66). When we recognize that the thought-world out of which James wrote was that of Jewish apocalyptic and not the later theologically-developed Christian eschatological perspective of the "last days" (as, for example, presented in Paul's epistles), we should not have much problem recognizing that the phrase "the Lord's coming" is parallel with the Old Testament's Day of God's judgment.

The language of James verses 1-6 is quite different from Paul's. James's words are an earlier way of expressing final judgment that are different from the way Paul expresses it. Paul's discussion of Christ's second coming gave to Christianity the technical and unique understanding of the event. But James's manner of speaking is more similar to the classical prophets and the Jewish apocalypticists when they spoke of the Day of Judgment. For example, when James invites the rich to weep and wail because of the miseries that are coming upon them (vs. 1), he was speaking like one of the prophets who announced the catastrophe that would come upon the wicked. The *Dies Irae* poem of Zephaniah is a classic example: "Wail you who live in the market district; all your merchants will be wiped out, all who trade with silver will be ruined. At that time I will search Jerusalem with lamps and punish those who are complacent . . . the great day of the Lord is near—near and coming quickly. Listen! The cry on the day of the Lord will be bitter. . . . That day will be a day of wrath, a day of distress and anguish, a day of trouble and ruin, a day of darkness and gloom, a day of clouds and blackness" (1:11-15).

Very significant is the fact that the judgment upon the rich is called a "day of slaughter" (James 5:5). This calls to mind the prophetic prediction of slaughter, carnage, and war that would be inflicted upon Jerusalem and the nations (see Jer. 25:34, which calls upon the nations to weep and wail for the day of slaughter; see also Ezek. 21:15; Isa. 35:2-4; Jer. 12:3).

James's judgment, then, parallels more the Old Testament judgment of local destruction rather than being a reference to the second coming. (Incidentally, it could be said that James's prediction occurred in A.D. 70 when Jerusalem was destroyed and the wealthy were slaughtered by the invading Romans as well as by the Zealots.) If James is not here speaking about the second coming, however, that fact does not lessen the truth of this basic Christian belief. A doctrine should not stand or fall upon the basis of one text. We must read each text in its context and allow the text to speak for itself. Inductive, rather than deductive, study is called for—exegesis (drawing out) rather than eisegesis (reading into).

Of interest is the fact that James's judgment on the rich is far more violent than anything found elsewhere in the New Testament (with the possible exception of Revelation 18). But this announcement of judgment brings hope and satisfaction to the poor and oppressed. There will be a great reversal: the powerful, rich exploiters will be destroyed, and the sufferers who waited patiently will receive the bountiful reward like the farmer.

"Patience" is the key idea in 5:7-11. James uses a different word for patience in verses 7, 8, 10 than he uses in verse 11. In the latter verse the word is the same as that in 1:2. The focus is on active perseverance. The word used in verses 7-10 (*makrothumeō* and its cognates) is usually used to indicate longsuffering. But the Latin American scholar Elsa Tamez has warned us that we should not understand James's use of the word in the traditional passive, negative sense. "The attitude is that of a waiting, as it were, on alert." She continues by noting that like the farmer "the oppressed community of James knows its difficult situation is going to change, that judgment has been pronounced in favor of those who suffer. It is important then that they do not despair" (55).

James illustrates his call to patience with the image of the small farmer (in contrast to the hired laborers in 5:4 who often had once been small farmers). The reference to autumn (October–November or December–January) and spring (March–April) rains point to a Palestinian provenance for the epistle—it's a natural local phenomenon with which the author was familiar. The farmer had to wait patiently for the autumn rains before sowing and then wait for the spring rains to ripen the crops. He had to wait for conditions outside his control. In this example from everyday life, James assures his poor, suffering community that even though their wait may be long, the judgment of the Lord on the rich is near and certain. This was good news for them. "The last word is not with those who provoke and frustrate. The last word is with the Lord" (Morris, 90).

Because James tells his readers to be patient, does this mean that we should make no effort to ameliorate social conditions around us now? I have noted elsewhere ("Poor and Rich," 256, 257) that it is widely held that the earliest Christians held to the view that Jesus was returning very soon and at that time he would bring judgment upon the wicked. It is believed by some that James held this view also. These persons suggest that because he saw his day as the last days and because he believed that the end was near, he did not demand social justice for the poor and oppressed who were victims of the rich exploiters. Since the old order of things will soon be swept away, reform and redress never entered James's mind. James's thinking, it is assumed, is similar to Paul's, who encouraged everyone to remain in his or her own social situation because of the imminence of the second coming (1 Cor. 7:17-26). Therefore, neither James nor Paul instigated social reform. In response to this argument, let us first recognize that James and Paul have different concerns. And neither should be imposed upon the other.

We must not conclude, then, that James is saying, like Paul is assumed to be implying, that the poor should remain in their pitiful social condition and nothing should be done about it by others who are more fortunate, because of the imminent advent. Besides, the use of Paul is specious, because it is doubtful that Paul would include the poor in the same social categories as slaves, virgins, and married persons (1 Cor. 7:17-26). On the contrary, Paul was quite proactive regarding the amelioration of poverty (Rom. 15:26; 2 Cor. 8, 9; Gal. 2:10).

In the second place, the point of James is not to address the role of nonsufferer vis-a-vis the poor under trial. In this passage, James is directly addressing only the sufferers—those who are being economically oppressed. His concern here is not with the ones who fall outside this category. I reckon, however, if James were here today, he would have a powerful word for those of us in positions of power and wealth to be involved in the amelioration of economic suffering around us. But in his context, James wishes to focus on those who are going through difficulties and disappointments, trials and tribulations. He says to them: Be patient; persevere.

In the midst of James's call for patience, he interjects a warning that seems at surface level to have nothing to do with his concern in this paragraph. He tells his readers: "Don't grumble against each other, brothers, or you will be judged. The Judge is standing at the door" (5:9). It is possible that this interruption of the flow of thought was occasioned by his focus on the day of judgment that will come upon the oppressive rich. But he wishes his readers to know that they also will be recipients of judgment if they are impatient and not longsuffering toward one another. Kistemaker is, therefore, correct, in my opinion, when he notes that "the people James addresses live in oppressive situations that cause them to lose patience with those who deprive them of basic necessities. In time, they become irritable toward those who share their miseries. They give vent to their repressed feelings and lash out at those who are close to them" (*James*, 166). James pleads with them to stop the grumbling.

Classic Examples of Patience

James returns specifically to the theme of patience in verses 10, 11 and gives specific examples to illustrate his point. He presents two examples of persons who have been patient and stood firm—the first is general, the second is specific.

The first is the example of the prophets (vss. 10, 11). Here James uses both words: patience (*makrothumias*) and perseverance (*hupomonēn*). These prophets were both longsuffering and they actively persevered. In the literary writings of the Old Testament and the intertestamental period, we encounter many instances in which prophets and men and women of God demonstrated these virtues. We are reminded of prophets, such as Elijah, who were patient and persevered in the face of trials and persecution. Even while being pursued by Jezebel, Elijah persevered (see 1 Kings 19). Amos in his conflict with Amaziah (Amos 7) and Jeremiah in his confrontation with King Zedekiah (Jer. 38) both endured patiently. Earlier we noted the perseverance of Mattathias and his son in their conflict with Antiochus Ephiphanes (1 Maccabees 2). And we should not ignore the fact that the "Hymn in honor of our ancestors" as found in Sirach 44-50 might have been at the back of James's mind. And although it is doubtful that Hebrews 11 influenced James's epistle, in this classic New Testament passage we find a rehearsal of other great persons and prophets who exemplified patience and perseverance under the most difficult circumstances. All these persons who persevered and endured James says are considered "blessed" (5:11). The implication should be clear to his readers: "You will be blessed [the second beatitude in the epistle; see 1:12] if you persevere" (see also Matt. 5:11, 12).

James's example of active patience is the story of Job. Job, as Sophie

Laws has noted, "was not a man under attack from others but one who experienced, albeit in an acute form, the ordinary human affliction of poverty, bereavement, and ill-health" (215). So even though Job's situation did not parallel the experience of James's community, James used him as an example of active perseverance. (We must note that the NIV's "perseverance" is a much better translation than the Authorized Version's "patience of Job," which has become a traditional phrase in English).

A careful reading of the Job narrative and poems as found in our canon raises the question as to whether or not he is truly an example of patience. A hundred years ago the well-known James commentator, Joseph B. Mayor, stated that "Job is not an example of what we should call patience except in his first acceptance of calamity (1:21; 2:10). We should rather say that his complaint in ch. 3, his indignation against his friends for their want of faith in him, his agony at the thought that God had forsaken him, were symptoms of an extremely sensitive, vehement, impatient character" (158). Others like William Barclay have noted that Job is portrayed in the Old Testament book as passionately resenting what had come upon him, "passionately questioning the conventional arguments of his so-called friends, passionately agonizing over the terrible thought that God might have forsaken him. Few men have spoken such passionate words" (125).

Because the canonical description of Job seems to be incompatible with James's evaluation of him, many have suggested that James is drawing on the depiction of Job as found in the intertestamental work called *The Testament of Job*. This book records the embellished versions of Job's experience, which were popular in Jewish circles. These stories emphasized the consummate patient endurance of Job under severe trials. In these accounts it is Job's wife, Sitis, who does the complaining, not Job. He is portrayed in a very positive light. He is also presented as a most righteous man who shared freely his wealth. Because of his patience and his great charity, he ultimately received God's praise and deliverance from his suffering.

Even though it is likely that *The Testament of Job* accounts were in James's mind, there is yet a sense in which the Old Testament account demonstrates the steadfastness of the ancient sage. Yes, he did complain bitterly about God and was very impatient with his friends, yet he never abandoned his faith and trust in God. Because of this perseverance, God blessed him abundantly and made him twice as prosperous as he had been before. Job lived to see his children unto the fourth generation (Job 42:10-17).

This is the patience and steadfast perseverance that James calls upon his community to possess in the midst of their suffering. Furthermore, in like manner (as in the case of Job), they will receive a sure blessing, because "the Lord is full of compassion and mercy" (5:11).

Swearing

James ends this subsection on patience with an admonition against swearing. On the surface there seems to be no connection with the preceding verses. Yet he does say at the beginning of verse 12, "Above all," intending to mean, "I don't want you to forget this point; it is very important." Although it is not clearly stated, it is possible that the stress and suffering led the poor in his community to be impatient and swear. It is important then, that James addresses this issue.

Swearing, here and in Jesus' statement in Matthew 5:34-37, should not be interpreted as the use of "dirty" language or profanity. Oath taking is what is being referred to. Both Jesus and James prohibit oath taking or swearing. Yet there seems to be clear evidence that such a prohibition is not as clear-cut in the rest of the Scriptures. Peter Davids has alerted us to the fact that "the swearing of oaths was limited in the OT to those which one would fulfil (Ex. 20:7; Lev. 19:12; Nu. 30:3). In some cases the swearing of oaths was commanded (Ex. 22:10, 11) or indeed done by God (Nu. 14:21; De. 4:31; 7:8). In the NT one can also find examples of oaths used or responded to by Jesus (Mt. 26:63) and by Paul (Rom 1:9; 1:20; 2 Cor. 1:23; 11:11; 1 Thes. 2:5, 10; Phil. 1:8). In the OT there is already a problem with using oaths too lightly (Je. 5:2; 7:9; Ho. 4:2; Zc. 5:3, 4; Mal. 3:5), and the warnings against oaths were later expanded into counsel to avoid oaths whenever possible so as to prevent their frivolous use (Sir. 23:9, 11)" (*Commentary*, 189).

By the time of Jesus and James, certain Jewish groups such as the Essenes, to whom we owe the Dead Sea Scrolls, totally renounced all oath taking, except at the initiation ceremony for a novice who was entering the community and in properly constituted court proceedings. Interestingly, the history of Christianity has shown that we have not practiced the rigor of Jesus' and James's prohibition regarding oath taking. Exceptions to this include the sixteenth-century Anabaptist reformers who refused to take oaths in the courtroom or in any other setting. The same is true of the Quakers who also took Jesus' and James's prohibition literally.

Neither James or Jesus are speaking to the issue of official oaths; rather, they are attacking the use of oaths in everyday discourse to prove one's integrity. The danger of the use of such oaths, says Burton Scott Easton, "is that men come to feel that if they are omitted, there is no binding necessity to speak the truth" (68). The focus, then, is on honesty and sincerity. This is what James calls his community to demonstrate. Even amidst the pain and suffering, they must be truthful and honest. Their Yes must be Yes, and their No No. They must say what they mean and mean what they say.

Gordon Poteat, in his homiletical exposition of James, has forcefully argued that the biblical emphasis on honesty and sincerity needs to be recaptured in our society. He has noted that "the opposite of honesty is deception and fraud. An American criminologist has stated that fraud is the most widespread criminal practice in our land, prevalent in respectable business circles as well as in the underworld. Is there not a widespread cynicism among us as to the reliability of the press, the advertisers, the lawyers, the politicians, or even the preachers?" (69). The call of James is to all of us—in the church as well as in society. The call is to truthfulness, honesty, and integrity. For James nothing, including suffering, should lessen the practice of such basic virtues.

■ Applying the Word

James 5:7-12

1. **When my suffering becomes so intense, do I tend to give up, or do I tend to hold on, steadfastly awaiting the Lord's solution? Can I think of a time when I reached the brink of**

ultimate despair but never stepped over? What was it that brought me back?

2. In an age when so much is "instant," how can I develop patience? In what specific circumstances in my life at this present time can I apply James's teaching on patience and perseverance?

3. Do I tend to be a grumbler or one who finds things for which to be joyful and thankful? If I fall into the first category, what steps can I take to move into the second?

■ Researching the Word

1. Use your concordance and find all the references you can to "rain" (early and latter) outside the book of James. Study each reference in its context (reading the verses prior and the verse after). Write down the context of each passage. Compare your findings with those of a Bible dictionary.

2. Use your concordance and find the words *oath* and *swear*. List in your notebook the times when they are commanded and the times they are not. Identify two or three instances when they proved disastrous. Compare your findings with the article(s) on these topics in a Bible dictionary or encyclopedia. What has this comparison done to enrich your understanding?

■ Further Study of the Word

1. For more on the interpretation of the "Lord's Coming" in 1:7, 8 as referring to the Old Testament "Day of the Lord," see P. Maynard-Reid, *Poverty and Wealth in James*, 95-98.

2. For an old but worthwhile study on the geography that informs James's writing, see D. Y. Hadidian, "Palestinian Pictures in the Epistle of James."

3. For a careful study of James's teaching regarding oaths and their relation to other biblical teaching on the same issue, see P. Davids, *Commentary on James*, 188-191.

CHAPTER ELEVEN

Prayer

James 5:13-20

James concludes his epistle by presenting his readers with the second response to suffering. In 5:7-12, the first response was a call for patience. The sufferer is urged to allow the Lord to take care of the judgment on the oppressors. Now James's thoughts turn to prayer. Another response to suffering—just as important as patience—is the discipline of prayer.

Prayer is the overriding theme of this section as evidenced in the fact that the word is mentioned in every verse, except the two concluding verses of the epistle (see vss. 13-18). Prayer here is both personal and communal. In trouble, joy, distress, and illness, the overarching response should be prayer. Whether the trials are physical, emotional, or economic, James is convinced the earnest prayer of a righteous person is powerful and effective.

■ Getting Into the Word

James 5:13-20

Read James verses 13-20 through twice prayerfully and thoughtfully. Then respond to the following questions and exercises:

1. Does 5:14, 15 also address the issue of public "faith healing" as practiced by many today? In your opinion, are all faith healers not of God? If No, what are the criteria in de-

termining which are of God and which are not? Is James
helpful here? Explain.

2. Does verse 15 mean that if a sick person is not healed, it is
   because there is a lack of faith? Is it because either the person praying for the sick one or the ill person himself or herself does not believe deeply enough that wholeness is not
   achieved? Explain.

3. Is the "confessing of sins" (vs. 16) a personal, private matter
   or a public event? If public (or both), are there some sins
   that should not be confessed publicly? If Yes, list the criteria
   you would use in determining which sins can be confessed
   in public and which ones should be confessed privately.

4. Compare the Elijah story in 1 Kings 17 and 18 with James
   5:17, 18. List the similarities and differences. Why did James
   choose this story to illustrate his point?

5. Compare and contrast verses 19, 20 with Matthew 18:15-
   17. Are there times when attempts to reconvert the sinner
   should not be made? If Yes, when would such a time be?
   Explain.

■ Exploring the Word

Responses to Trouble, Happiness, and Sickness

If anyone is in "trouble," instead of swearing (5:12) or impatiently
taking things into his or her own hands (vs. 7), James exhorts that
person to pray (vs. 13). The "trouble" in verse 13 should not be limited to sickness (as one may be tempted to do after reading the passage); James will get to that specific type of suffering in just a moment. This misfortune or distress parallels the suffering in 2 Timothy
2:8, 9 in which Paul is cited as saying "This is my gospel, for which
I am suffering even to the point of being chained." The same Greek
word is used here for "trouble" (*kakopatheō*; see also James 5:10).
The emphasis is more on spiritual and emotional distress (Hayden,
258, 263). These were difficult times. James's community was suffering at the hands of the oppressive rich. His epistle was written

during volatile times. Zealot activities were increasing and widespread. Was James attempting to defuse the situation? Yes, but he was not simply calling for a laid-back, passive response to the misfortunes and hardships of the time; he called for a positive response. He rejected the "attack-fire-with-fire" method as well as the resignation *modus operandi* of the Stoics. Instead, James calls upon his readers to pray.

This exhortation reminds us of Jesus saying to His disciples, as He told them the parable of the persistent widow, "that they should always pray and not give up" (Luke 18:1; compare Paul's imperative: "Pray in the Spirit on all occasions"—Eph. 6:18; 1 Thess. 5:17). Like Jesus and Paul, James's emphasis is most likely on persistence. He does not let us know that the content of the prayer should be: Should it include requests for the removal of trouble? Or should it be a seeking for strength to endure it? Or maybe both? James doesn't say. All he says is to pray. Sincere prayer is powerful and effective whatever the content (vs. 16).

Although James's overriding concern is the theme of suffering, he inserts a joyful line: "Is anyone happy? Let him sing songs of praise" (vs. 13). The word for "happy" (*euthumeō*) includes more than being outwardly happy. Its reference is to an emotion that is not dependent on external circumstances and prevailing conditions. It is "the cheerfulness and happiness of heart that one can have whether in good times or in bad. It was this sense of well-being that Paul encouraged his fellow travelers to have even though their ship was in imminent danger of destruction (Acts 27:22, 25)" (Moo, 175, 176).

As evidence of this inner joy, James exhorts his readers to express it outwardly by "singing songs of praise." The Greek word from which this phrase is translated is *psallō*. It can indicate playing the harp or singing a capella. R. V. G. Tasker notes that this word from which our English word *psalm* is derived "originally meant to play by touching a stringed instrument, and then to sing to the accompaniment of the harp" (128). Whether with instruments or without, the call is for joyful expression. James does not say whether these expressions should be private or public singing "and making melody in your heart to the Lord" as Paul commanded (Eph. 5:19, KJV).

But the overall context of the passage suggests that both the prayer of the one in trouble as well as the music of the joyful person should be expressed privately as well as in the public community.

From the general trouble and distress of 5:13, James next focuses on a specific type of suffering: sickness. The context seems to indicate that the illness is serious and not a transient malady or ordinary indisposition. The fact is that the ill person is possibly incapable of leaving his or her residence, thus the elders have to be summoned. It is because the Christian church has for centuries accepted this verse as speaking to extreme illness that the *SDA Bible Commentary* notes that "by the 8th century this passage of Scripture had come to be used in support of the practice of what Catholics today call extreme unction, or the last rites of the church for the dying. The Council of Trent in its fourteenth session, 1551, officially declared that James here teaches the sacramental efficacy of the oil" (Nichol, ed., 7:540). James, however, does not tell us how ill a person must be before he summons the elder. What he does say is that when a person reaches a point of sickness (with which his readers most likely were well acquainted), the elders should be called to pray. This is quite unlike the command in the previous verse in which the individual is to pray for himself or herself. Here our author urges the ill one to avail himself or herself of the prayer of another.

The question arises at this point: Who are the "elders" whose designated task it is to perform the anointing? Because of the qualifying phrase "of the church," it is naturally assumed that these are leaders of the Christian community, similar to those in Acts 11:30; 15:2, 4, 6, 23; and 20:17, 28. In these passages, the elders are either mentioned along with the apostles or leaders in the early church, or later as overseers and pastors of the church.

If James, as we have argued, was written before the church had fully separated from Judaism and before such offices as elders were developed exclusively for Christians, and if James's epistle was intended for a wider audience than simply a small body of believers in Jerusalem, then "elders" may have a wider connotation. It is possible that James is speaking of the older men in the various local assemblies (*ekklēsia*, traditionally translated as "church"), Jewish or Christian, synagogue or Christian house-church (Easton, 15, 16; Adamson, *The Epistle*, 197; Martin, 207). But for the most part, James's concern is quite different from ours. We focus on who should perform a particular ceremony; James focuses on what should be done.

There are two things that should be done. First, visit the sick and pray for him or her. Second, "anoint him with oil in the name of the Lord" (5:14). In the first place, visiting the sick was highly esteemed in Judaism and by Jesus. In Jesus' final parable in Matthew's Gospel, He speaks of salvation coming to those who visited the sick (Matt. 25:36). Prior to Christ, ben Sirach wrote, "Do not hesitate to visit the sick, because for such deeds you will be loved" (Sir. 7:35, NRSV). Later, we find in the Jewish Talmud: "He who visits the sick, should not merely sit on a bed or on a chair, but he should wrap himself in his cloak and implore God to take pity on the sick person" (Shabboth 13, cited in Kugelman, 64). Similar to this passage and the one in James is the Baba Batra 116a: "Let him into whose house calamity or sickness has come, go to a wise man (i.e., a rabbi) that he may intercede for him with God" (Ropes, 304).

The visiting elder must do more than pray. Anointing with oil is enjoined. What the purpose is of this anointing James does not enlighten us. If it were a widespread practice in New Testament times, we have little record of that fact. Only here in James, in Mark 6:13 (where the disciples returned from their missionary journey having anointed people with oil and healed them), and in Luke 10:34 (where the Good Samaritan poured oil and wine on the wounds of the beaten traveler) do we find references to such a practice. This does not diminish the speculation as to the purpose of the anointing. There are generally two suggested possibilities.

The first possibility is practical and therapeutic. Oil was widely used in the ancient world for medicinal purposes; for healing, soothing, and cleansing (see Isa. 1:6; Luke 10:34). Philo, the Jewish philosopher, said that olive oil "produces smoothness, and counteracts physical exhaustion, and brings about good condition. If a muscle be relaxed it braces it and renders it firm, nor is there anything surpassing it for infusing tone and vigour" (Dibeluis, 252 n. 63). Herod the Great, as he lay dying, was urged by his physicians to take a bath in oil (Josephus, *Wars of the Jews*, I. 33.5; noted in Mayor, 165). The medicinal properties of oil were also praised by other ancients such as Galen ("for paralysis") and Pliny ("for toothache") (noted in Laws, 227).

Questions, however, are raised as to whether or not James had in mind the therapeutic view. If the intent was medicinal, why were elders of the church called? Why not relatives or physicians? With these questions in mind, others have suggested a second possibility; namely, a symbolic religious rite. Peter Davids thus states that oil is not here used as a medicine but "rather it is an outward and physically perceptible sign of the spiritual power of prayer, as well as a sign of authority of the healer" (*James*, 123). Others suggest that it symbolizes God's concern for the sick one, His trustworthiness, and is a symbolic demonstration of His special care and attention (Moo, 179; R. P. Martin, 208).

An either/or distinction seems to be an incorrect conclusion. I agree with Sophie Laws that "it would . . . be wrong to distinguish between the 'medical' and 'religious' elements of James's picture. A distinction between remedies based on superstition [or religious faith] and remedies based on science would have been foreign even to the practitioners of Greek medicine" (227), much less to a Jewish audience such as the one James is addressing. The oil, then, was used practically to bring healing and/or relief of pain, but its application was based on the belief that the Divine hand was at work. That is why it was done "in the name of the Lord" (5:14).

Healing in the name of the Lord must not be associated with the magical or mechanical invocation of God's name, the name of Jesus, or the many other names that were called upon during healing and exorcist ceremonies in the first century. James is simply stating the grounds upon which the healing is achieved. It is through God's power the sick will find wholeness.

Before leaving this section, we should note that the elders are called to pray "over" the sick person. This suggests to some that hands were laid upon the ill person when prayer was being offered and that certain power emanates through the healer. James, however, does not describe the situation thus. It should be noted that it is the leaders as a group who are called to pray over the sick and to do the anointing. James is not here describing the practice of faith-healing by an individual as is widely practiced today. This is not to rule out the possibility of God working through individuals in a faith-healing enterprise. However, verse 14 should not be used as a proof text to validate such a charismatic gift.

Salvation, Forgiveness, Confession, and Healing

Let us not be sidetracked regarding James's focus. It is neither the anointing with oil nor is it the laying on of hands. His emphasis is on prayer. Thus he begins verse 15 with the words, "And the prayer offered in faith will make the sick person well." Here a new dimension is mentioned: faith. James is not talking about any and every prayer. Only the prayer of "faith." Nor does he imply that the frequency or fervency of prayer will bring about the desired results. It is faith that renders the prayer effective. James does not explicitly say whose faith is intended here. But since the context indicates it is the elders who offer up the prayer (vs. 14), most likely their faith is intended.

The Authorized Version translates the word *well* ("make the sick person well") as *save*. The word *sōzō* ("save") is not exclusively a religious term. Its basic meaning is to rescue, to deliver, to restore. The same is true for the word *raise up* (*egeirō*). Neither of these words should be limited to final salvation and the resurrection from the dead. James is speaking here of physical restoration and wholeness here and now. Yet even though this might be his primary intent, we must not eliminate the religious dimension. In the Jewish mind, physical healing and personal salvation go hand in hand.

The certainty of the future tense in verse 15 ("*will* make the sick person well," "*will* raise him up," "*will* be forgiven") has led some to wonder how absolutely we should take these words—especially the first and second phrases. Some have solved the problem by arguing that the statement was confined to the apostolic age and it should not be taken as an infallible assurance today. There is nothing, of course, in the text that limits it thus. Others have limited the text by understanding it to be saying, "The Lord will make the sick well *if He deems it best*." The *SDA Bible Commentary* pursues this position when it states that "restoration to health in answer to prayer may be immediate or may be a gradual process. It may come about directly by a divine act that transcends man's finite knowledge of natural law, or it may come about indirectly—and more gradually—by divine guidance in the application of natural remedies. The latter process is no less an answer to prayer than the former, and is as truly a mani-festation of divine love, wisdom, and power. The mature Christian will recognize that God does not do for a man what he may do for himself or what others may do for him. The mature Christian will realize that divine love and wisdom do not, at least as a rule, make supernatural provision for what can be accomplished by natural means, through the intelligent application of known scientific prin-ciples" (Nichol, ed., 7:541). Theologically, this is orthodox. Yet can we impose this understanding on James in *this* context? Possibly we should simply accept R. A. Martin's suggestion that the phrase "will save" "is best understood here, as a forceful way of saying that it is prayer and the power God chooses to make available in response to prayer that accomplishes this healing" (48, 49).

James ties sin and sickness together when he states, "If [the sick person] has sinned, he will be forgiven. Therefore confess your sins to each other and pray for each other so that you may be healed" (vss. 15, 16). In the ancient world, sin and sickness went hand in hand. The case of Job, who was accused by his friends of being sin-ful, and thus responsible for his own sickness, illustrates this (com-pare Job 4:1–5:27) as does the Johannine narrative regarding the man who was born blind. In this latter case, the disciples asked Jesus: "Who sinned, this man or his parent?" (John 9:2). However, both the case of Job as well as Jesus' response to the disciples ("Neither this man nor his parents sinned"—John 9:3) make it clear that there is not a strict biblical equation between sin and sickness. James, how-ever, implies that some illnesses are connected with sin.

If some illnesses are related to sin, then it is logical that confes-sion and forgiveness are imperative. This is indicated in the words of the Jewish rabbis and Jesus. The former believed that before a person could be healed, his sins had to be forgiven. Rabbi Alexandrai said, "No man gets up from his sickness until God has forgiven him all his sins" (Barclay, 131). And as Jesus healed the paralytic, He said, "Son, your sins are forgiven" (Mark 2:5).

What types of sin necessitate confession and forgiveness? It seems obvious that some sins related to health are included in this category. Thus the *SDA Bible Commentary* suggests James is referring to sins that include "departures from known principles of healthful living." These sins "are freely forgiven on the basis of divine mercy and the sick man's determination henceforth to live in harmony with known health principles" (Nichol, ed., 7:541). This suggestion has more validity than the opinion that "the *faults* he has chiefly in mind are offences against other brethren, which spoil their fellowship with one another and make it difficult, if not impossible, for them to worship together as the people of God [cf. Matt. 5:23, 24]" (Tasker, 135). In this latter suggestion, there is no hint of illness or suffering. James's concern is with the sick. Yet we are not even sure that James's interest is primarily with departures from healthful living. What we are sure of is that in James's theology, wholeness of body is tied in with wholeness of soul. Thus confession and forgiveness are important prerequisites of healing.

An additional word should be said on the matter of confession. James admonishes that the confession should be made "to each other" (5:16). This seems to suggest a public setting. Some may take this as a command to make public confession of sins a mandate in the church. But "it is not a legitimate inference from this passage to suppose that James is exhorting his readers either to make public confession of *all* their sins without restraint to their fellow Christians in a general assembly, or to unbosom themselves *completely* even to chosen individuals in private" (Tasker, 135). I have personally seen this type of extreme adoption of the text do more harm than good. We must seek wisdom to know when public confession of sins is helpful and not harmful in the process of wholeness.

James underlines his emphasis on prayer by pointing out that "the prayer of a righteous man is powerful and effective" (vs. 16). It is interesting that he did not say "a righteous elder." The effective prayer is not restricted to a special class of persons who have a monopoly on the line between heaven and earth. Nor should "righteous" be interpreted as "free from mistakes," "sinless," "perfect." This verse not only serves to conclude this section on prayer, healing, and confession but serves as an introduction to the example of Elijah. Elijah is not portrayed in the Old Testament as sinlessly perfect. But he is presented as a person who was in active fellowship, communion, and relationship with God—i.e., one who was righteous in the Old Testament sense of the word. The prayer of any such person involved in that type of righteous relationship is powerful and effective.

The Example of Elijah

In bringing forth Elijah as an example of effectual prayer, James first makes the vitally important point that he was "just like us" (vs. 17). The Greek word, *homoiopathēs*, from which this phrase is translated, suggests that Elijah had the same limitations that all human beings possess. "In Jewish tradition, as in the Old Testament," says Peter Davids, "Elijah is very human. He is godly, but often falls prey to doubts and depression. . . . [He is] an ordinary man with an extraordinary God" (*James*, 125). James is attempting to let his readers understand that what Elijah did was not accomplished through some superhuman, extraordinary, magical performance. He was a person, just like ourselves, who had access to the Divine. Our prayers can be just as effective as his.

It may be of interest to note that the incident referred to here is recorded in 1 Kings 17 and 18. However, James is not totally dependent on that record for his account. The Old Testament narrative does not say anything about the length of the drought being three years, nor does it report that the cessation of rain was in response to prayer. It seems more than likely that these added data were gained from rabbinic sources (note also Luke 4:25) that portrayed popular understanding of the story. In rabbinic exegesis, evidence for Elijah's prayer was extrapolated from the fact that Elijah stood before God (1 Kings 17:1) and later threw himself on the earth and placed his face between his knees (18:42; see R. A. Martin, 49; Moo, 188).

It is also Jewish exegesis that gives us the three-and-a-half-year duration for the drought. In Jewish prophetic and apocalyptic writings, three and a half (half of the perfect number seven) was in many instances the length of time for a period of disaster and judgment (Dan. 7:25; 12:7; Rev. 11:2; 12:14). Bo Reicke also notes that this time frame "may be interpreted as a period of waiting for the final manifestation of God's grace" (61). Whatever its meaning might be in James's community, the fact is that James uses it to serve to encourage his readers who are undergoing severe suffering that they could be confident that just as Elijah's prayer was efficacious, so their fervent prayer in the time of their distress would avail much.

Conclusion

James concludes his letter with two verses (5:19, 20), which at first glance seem to have no tie with the preceding verses. Yet, when he speaks of wandering from the truth and someone bringing back the wanderer, we sense that he is reverting to verses 15, 16, where he spoke of forgiveness and confession. On the other hand, these verses could be viewed as a concluding statement to the entire epistle. The wandering persons would then be those who find themselves participating in the negative activities he has addressed throughout the letter.

The final admonitions have roots in the Old Testament and (as should be expected by now) in later Jewish literature. In the first place, they bring to mind the ancient proverb: "Whoever says to the guilty, 'You are innocent'—people will curse him and nations denounce him. But it will go well with those who convict the guilty, and rich blessing will come upon them" (Prov. 24:24, 25). It also resembles the direction and ethos of the Qumran community by the Dead Sea (R. P. Martin, 217).

The parallels with Matthew's record of Jesus' words concerning "the brother who sins against you" (18:15-17) is striking, if the Matthean text is interpreted correctly. Although Jesus' words were not related to someone who wanders from "truth," His focus was on how that one should be treated, loved, and kept or brought back into fellowship. The sinner should be treated as a "pagan [i.e., Gentile] or a tax collector" (18:17). Jesus' treatment of these classes of persons was not disfellowship and disregard. He treated them with love, acceptance, and forgiveness. (Notice immediately afterward He told Peter to forgive them seventy-seven times or seventy times seventy—18:21, 22.)

In James's case, however, the one who wanders has wandered from "the truth." It is popularly believed that "truth" is orthodoxy (i.e. truth that is believed). However, for James, truth is not so much orthodoxy but orthopraxis (truth that is lived). Truth is a way of life, not mere assent to intellectual facts (see 2:14-26). The final call of James, therefore, is an admonition for his readers to help those who are not *living* the truth to turn from their evil ways. This radical conversion will, in a proactive way, relieve the pain of those who are suffering due to the errors and sins of the wanderer.

■ Applying the Word

James 5:13-20

1. James says in 5:13 "Is anyone happy? Let him sing songs of praise." Has modernism taken over my life to the extent that rather than sing I tend to *listen* to singing? How can I go about reviving singing in my personal or family worship? Or how can I go about beginning the act of singing for the first time?

2. Do I find that pastoral calls to church members who are sick or suffering are less than they used to be? How can I encourage my local congregation to be more active in such visitations?

3. How has my knowledge of modern science (e.g., meteorology) made me skeptical of praying for things like rain? How can I be true to science and at the same time have a strong prayer life?

4. What have I done in the past twelve months to bring back someone who has wandered from the truth? What plans do I have to assist in the restoration of "sinners" in my community within the next year?

■ Researching the Word

1. Using a concordance, find in Scripture eight to ten other examples of answered prayers that were not mentioned in this chapter of the commentary. Can you find two to three that were not answered positively? Why do you think they were not?
2. With the help of your concordance, find all the references in the Bible to periods of three and a half days, months, years, etc. What is the context of each? Can you find any other symbolic meaning to these periods besides that which was noted in the "Exploring the Word" section above? What are they?

■ Further Study of the Word

1. For an interpretive study of what James said regarding healing, what he did *not* say, and what all this means for our modern situation, see J. Wilkerson's "Healing in the Epistle of James."
2. For general insights and exhortations regarding the use of prayer in bringing wholeness, see E. G. White, *Ministry of Healing*, the chapter entitled "Prayer for the Sick," 225-233.